Samsung Galaxy

S21 Ultra 5G

User Manual

A Comprehensive Pictorial Illustrative Guide For Operating Your New S21 Series

BY

Jean R. T. Luc

Table of Contents

CHAPTEFR ONE

THE NEW AND IMPROVED FEATURES

S PEN (S21 ULTRA 5G ONLY)

S pen

The S pen (sold separately). The S Pen offers a variety of useful features. Use the S Pen to launch applications, capture or draw an image.

Some features of the S Pen, such as tapping the touch screen, may not work if the device is close to a magnet.

Aerial view

Hold the S Pen across the screen to view the contents or view product information on the screen.

The following Air view features are available:

- ✓ Check your email before opening.
- ✓ View the contents of the photo album or enlarge the image.
- ✓ Watch a video and jump to a specific scene by scrolling above the timeline.

✓ See the name or description of the icon or button.

NOTE The preview function is only available if the pointer on the S Pen screen is continuous.

Off-screen note

You can write notes without turning on the screen.

1. When the screen is off, press the S Pen button and touch the screen.

2. Touch to customize the note:

- ❖ Color: change the color of the stylus.
- ❖ Pen settings: Touch to use the pen tool. Double-tap to adjust the line thickness.
- ❖ Eraser: Touch to use the eraser. Double-tap to delete everything.

3. Touch Save to save the note in Samsung Notes. NOTE The off-screen note setting must be enabled

Pinto always displayed Note

You can pin or edit a note that is always displayed.

1. On the off-screen note, tap Attach to always display it.

2. Touch Attach to always displayed.

Air Command Access S Pen signature functions from any screen, including Smart select, Screen write, and Samsung Notes.

1. Touch the air command or hold down the S Pen near the screen so that the cursor appears, and then press the S Pen button once.

2. Touch:

Create note: Launch a new note in Samsung Notes.

- View all notes: launch the Samsung Notes application and see the list of created notes
- Smart selection: draw an area of the screen to collect it in the Gallery application.
- Screensaver: Take screenshots and write or draw them.
- Live messaging: Create a short animated message by drawing or writing with a stylus.
- AR doodle: draw interactive doodle logos using the AR camera function.
- Translate: move the mouse pointer over a word to view it translated into another language and listen to its pronunciation.
- **PENUP**: Use the S Pen to draw, edit, and share live drawings or images.
- Add shortcuts: add more applications or functions to the Air Command menu.
- Settings: Customize the air command by configuring applications and features

and changing the way the air command menu is displayed.

Creating a note

Start a new note directly in the Samsung Notes application.

Touch Air Command> Create Note.

View all notes

Launch the Samsung Notes application and see the list of created notes.

○ Touch Air Command> Show All Notes.

Smart selection

The smart selection feature allows you to copy content from any screen. You can then add it to the Gallery app or share it with your contacts.

1. Touch Air Command> Smart Select.

2. Touch a shape in the menu, then drag S Pen to select the content. The following options appear:

> ❖ Extract text: Recognize and extract text from the selected content.
> ❖ Screen anchors: set a shortcut to the collected content on the home screen.

- ❖ Automatic selection: Allow smart selection to automatically select the content you want to select.
- ❖ Drawing: Draw on recorded content.
- ❖ Share: select a sharing method to share your content.

3. Touch Save.

TIP Tap Animation to record an animation, or Pinto screen to pin content to the Smart select screen.

Screen saver The screen saver allows you to take screenshots and write or draw on them.

1. Touch Air Command> Screen Saver.

2. The current screen is saved and the pen tool is displayed.

The following editing tools are available:

- ✓ Crop: Drag the edges of the screen to crop the recorded content.
- ✓ Pen type: draw a screen image. Second, tap the stylus icon to change the tip, size, and color of the stylus.
- ✓ Eraser: delete a note or drawing from the screenshot.
- ✓ Undo: Undo the last action.
- ✓ Repeat: repeat the last canceled action.

✓ Share: select a sharing method to share your content.

3. Touch Save. The content is saved in the Gallery application.

TIP Hold down the Pen button to delete drawings on the screen.

Live Messages

Record an animated drawing or a written message.

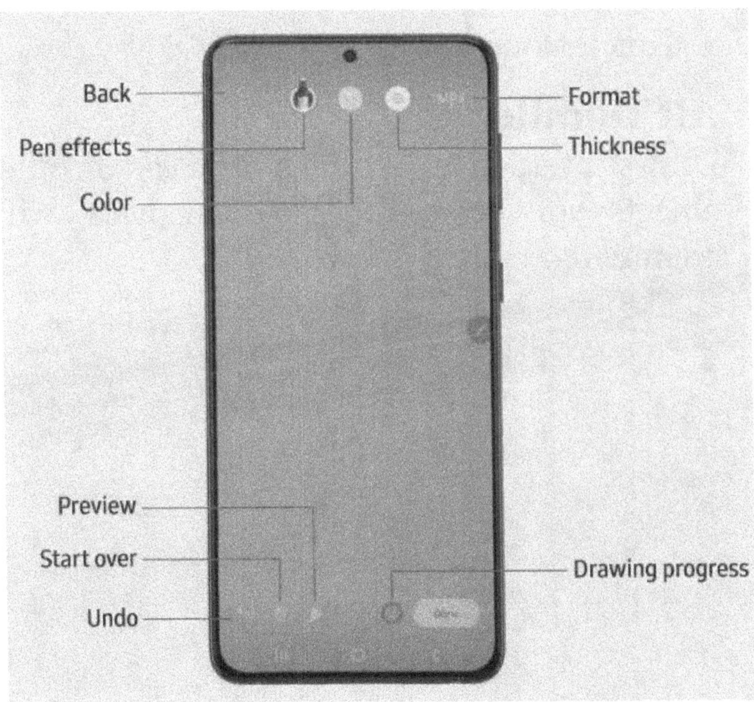

1. Touch Air Command> Live Messaging.

7

2. In the background, select one of the following options:

- Collection: View all the messages you have created live.

- Gallery: Select a picture or video as wallpaper.

- Camera: Take a background image. l Color: Select a background color.

3. Follow the instructions to start creating a live message.

4. Touch Done to save.

AR Doodle

Draws interactive logo logs on faces or other objects you see through the camera, with augmented reality.

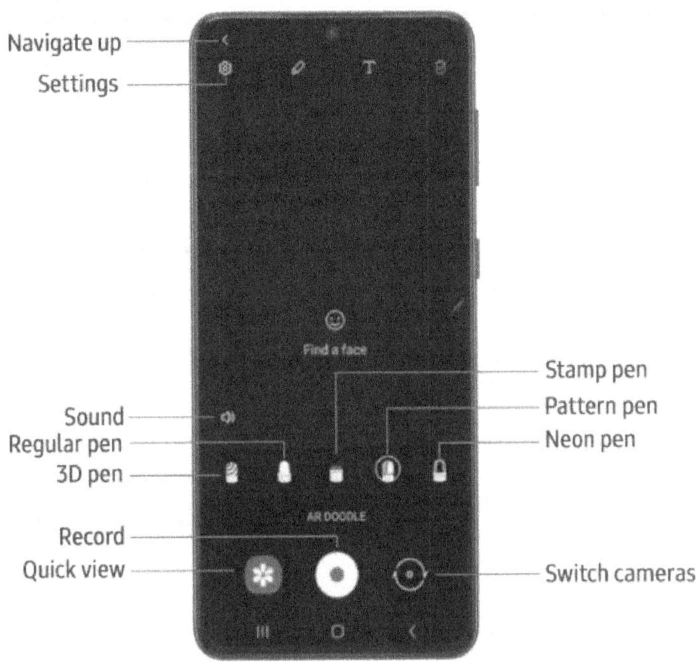

1. Touch Air command> AR Doodle.

2. Touch Switch Camera to select the front or rear camera.

3. Position the camera with your target in the center of the screen.

4. Use the S Pen to draw.

- The Doodle logo monitors facial movements in real-time.

5. Touch Record to save the video of your AR Doodle.

Translate

Move the mouse pointer over the words with the S Pen to translate them and listen to their pronunciation.

1. Tap Air Command> Translate.

2. Touch the source and target languages to change them to the desired language.

3. Move the mouse pointer over one word.

- Touch Sound to hear a word spoken in the original language.
- Touch Copy to save the selected text and translation.

4. Touch Close to close Translator.

PENUP

Use the S Pen to draw, edit and share live images.

Touch Air Command> PENUP.

Adding Shortcuts

You can customize the Air command menu by adding shortcuts to applications and features.

1. Touch Air Command> Add Shortcuts.

2. Touch the applications or features you want to add to the Air command menu.

- To remove a shortcut to an application, tap Remove.

3. Touch Navigation Up to save the selection.

Configuring S Pen Settings

To configure S Pen settings:

- In Settings, tap Advanced Features> S Pen to configure the following settings:

- Notes screen: Create notes without turning on the screen. Notes from the external display are saved in Samsung Notes.

- Create a note with the Pen button: Press and hold the Pen button, then double-tap the Pen screen to start a new note.

- Air view: switch on or off Air view.

- Show the pointer while hovering: turn the pointer on or off. The cursor appears on the screen when the tip of the S stylus is close to the screen, indicating available actions.

Air Command

-Shortcuts: Configure the Air command menu with S Pen functions, applications, and functions.

- Show floating icon: Displays an air command icon that you can use to move around the screen.

- Open the Air Command with the Pen Button: Open the Air Command menu when you point to the pointer above the screen and press the Pen button.

Feedback

- Sound: Set the machine to emit sounds when writing to the screen.

General

-Tips for using the S Pen: Learn how to use the functions of the S Pen.

- About S Pen functions: See the S Pen version information.

- Contact us: Contact Samsung support through Samsung members (if supported by your operator).

CHAPTER TWO

MOBILE CONTINUITY

Mobility continuously Access device memory and other features on compatible mobile devices and computers.

Connecting to Windows

Achieve uninterrupted mobility between your Samsung device and your Windows computer. By connecting devices, you can instantly access photos, messages, and more on your computer.

Pictures

- ✓ Drag and drop pictures into Windows.
- ✓ Open and edit images in the photo application.
- ✓ Share pictures with contacts via Windows.

✓ Messaging (SMS / MMS)

- ✓ Support for group MMS messages.
- ✓ Integration with Windows Emoji Picker.
- ✓ When you receive a new message, you get a Windows pop-up window.

Notifications

    I.   Look and manage phone notifications from your computer.

   II.   Exclude notifications from some phone applications.

 III.   When you receive a new notification, you get a Windows pop-up window.

To Mirror Apps

    a. Stream your phone's screen live on your computer.

    b. Communicate with your phone using the keypad and mouse.

    c. Use Windows accessibility.

To connect your device to your computer

1. In Settings, tap Advanced Features> Connect to Windows.

2. Follow the instructions to connect the device to the computer.

TIP You can also enable this feature in the Quick Settings menu.

SAMSUNG DeX

Connect your device to your PC or TV for enhanced multitasking.

    ✓ Send DeX to the TV and continue using the device or change it to a touchpad.

  ✓ Connect to a TV or monitor wirelessly or with an HDMI cable.

  ✓ Download DeX to your computer for quick and easy file transfers.

Enabling DeX

1. In Settings, tap Advanced Features> Samsung DeX.

2. Touch to turn on the function.

3. Follow the instructions on the device to connect to the TV or computer.

  ✓ If you are connecting to a computer, download the DeX application to your computer at samsungdex.com.

Continuing apps on other devices

This feature allows you to make and receive calls and text messages from Galaxy devices that are signed in to your Samsung account.

1. In Settings, tap Advanced Features> Continue Apps on Other Devices.

2. Touch to turn on the function. The connection is made automatically.

3. Log in to your Samsung account on Galaxy devices.

TIP Move your contacts from your device to your Samsung account so that you can access them on all registered devices.

CHAPTER THREE

BIXBY

What is Bixby

Bixby is a user interface that helps you use the device more easily. You can voice to Bixby or type text. Bixby will launch the feature you are requesting or display the information you want.

Starting Bixby

Press and hold the side key to start Bixby. Bixby's introductory page will appear.

After selecting the language to use with Bixby, log in to your Samsung account and complete the setup following the on-screen instructions,

the Bixby screen will appear.

Using Bixby

When you press and hold the side button, tell Bixby what you want, then release your finger from the button.

Alternatively, say hello to Bixby and say what you want.

For example, when you press and hold the side key, say What time is it today?

The weather information is displayed on the screen.

If you want to know tomorrow whether, click and hold the side button, just talk Tomorrow?

If Bixby asks you a question during a call while answering Bixby while pressing and holding the side key. Or tap Bixby and respond to it.

If you're using a Bluetooth headset or audio device, or start a conversation by saying "Hello, Bixby," you can continue the conversation without touching the icon.

Launch the Bixby app and press - Automatic Listening Hands-free only.

Awakening Bixby by Voice

You can start a conversation with Bixby by saying "Hi, Bixby." Register your voice so Bixby will respond to your voice when you say "Hi, Bixby."

1 Launch the Bixby application and press →ic Voice wake-up.

2 Touch the Wake switch with Hi, Bixby to activate it.

3 Follow the on-screen directives to complete the installation.

Now you can say "Hi, Bixby" and start the conversation.

Communicating by typing text

If your speech or voice is hard to recognize due to a noisy environment, you can communicate with Bixby through text.

Launch the Bixby app, tap, and then enter what you want.

During communication, Bixby will also respond via text instead of voice feedback.

Bixby Vision
what is Bixby vision

Bixby Vision is a service that offers a variety of features based on image recognition.

You can use Bixby Vision to quickly search for information by identifying objects.

Use the various useful features of Bixby Vision.

• This function may not be available or you may not get accurate search results depending on the image size, shape, or resolution.

• Samsung is not responsible for the product information offered by Bixby Vision.

Starting Bixby Vision

Start Bixby Vision using one of these methods.

- In the Camera app, tap MORE in the list of shooting modes and tap BIXBY VISION.
- In the gallery, select a picture and tap.
- In a web application, tap and hold an image, then tap Search with Bixby Vision.
- If you have added the Bixby Vision application icon to the application screen, launch the Bixby Vision application.

Using Bixby Vision

1 Start Bixby Vision.

2 Choose the function you need.

- ✓ Recognizes text from documents or images and translates it.
- ✓ Search for images similar to a recognized object on the network and related information.
- ✓ Search for product information.
- ✓ Recognize QR codes and view information.
- ✓ The available features and search results may vary by region or service provider.

Bixby Routines

Add repetitive usage patterns as routines and make your device more enjoyable.

For example, a "bedtime routine" will perform actions, such as turning on a silent and dark way to keep your eyes and ears from shaking when you use the device before bed.

Adding Routines

1 Open the Settings app and click Advanced features → Bixby routines.

2 In the Discover list, select the routine you want or tap Add routines to add your routines.

- You can set routine conditions and actions in the Discover list.
- To set the routine status manually, tap the Start button.

This option only appears if no operating conditions are set.

When a pop-up window appears, tap Add. You can add a routine to the home screen as an add-on and access it quickly.

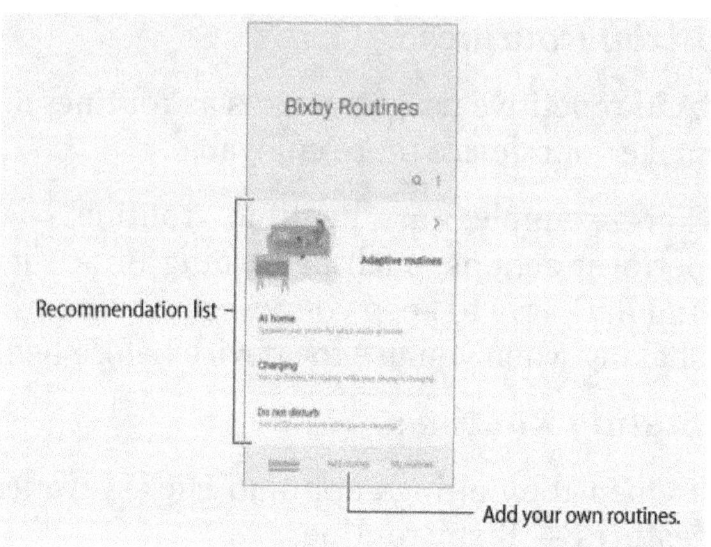

Adding recommended routines

Once the device has learned your usage patterns, it will recommend adding useful or frequently used features as a routine.

When a recommendation notification appears, tap Show all and add it as your routine.

Starting Automatic Routines

Automatic routines start automatically when their conditions are detected.

Performing manual routines

For manual routines that are set to operate conditions by pressing the Start button, you can start them manually by tapping the button at any time.

Open the Settings app and click Advanced Features - Bixby Routines -My Routines and click next to the routine you want to run.

Alternatively, click the routine program on the Home screen.

Viewing running routines

Currently, running routines appear in the notification panel. To view routine details, tap the notification.

You can also quickly stop running routines. In the notification pane, click next to routine and tap Stop.

Managing Routines

Open the Settings app and click Advanced features >Bixby routines > My routines.

Your routines will be displayed.

To disable a routine, click Routine >Disable this routine.

To delete routines, press > Delete, highlight the routines you want to delete, and tap Delete.

CHAPTER FOUR

BIOMENTRY SECURITY

Use biometrics to securely unlock your device and sign in to your accounts.

Face Detection

You can enable face recognition to unlock the screen. To unlock the device with your face, you need to set a pattern, PIN, or password.

- ❖ Face recognition is less protective than a pattern, PIN, or password. The device may unlock someone or something similar to your image.
- ❖ Some conditions can affect face recognition, including wearing glasses, a hat, a beard, or heavy makeup.
- ❖ When registering a face, make sure you are in a well-lit place and that the camera lens is clean.

1. In Settings, c;ick Biometrics & Security> Face Detection.

2. Follow the face registration instructions.

Face Detection Control

Adjust the face detection work.

- In Settings, tap Biometrics & Security> Face Detection.

Remove face data: delete existing faces.

- ✓ Add an alternate look: Improve face recognition by adding an alternate look.
- ✓ Face Unlock: Enable or disable face detection security.
- ✓ Stay on the lock screen until you drag: When you unlock the face recognition device, stay on the lock screen until you drag the screen.
- ✓ Faster recognition: switch on for faster face detection. Switch it off to improve security and make it harder to unlock with a picture like.
- ✓ Request open eyes: Face detection only recognizes your face when your eyes are open.
- ✓ Brighten the screen: Temporarily increase the brightness of the screen so that your face can be recognized in dark conditions.
- ✓ About biometric unlocking: Read more about protecting your device with biometric data.

Fingerprint Scanner

Use fingerprint recognition as an alternative to entering passwords in some applications.

You can also use your fingerprint to verify your identity when you sign in to your Samsung account.

To unlock the device with your fingerprint, you need to set a pattern, PIN, or password.

1. In Settings, tap Biometrics & Security> Fingerprints.

2. Follow the instructions for registering your fingerprints.

Manage Fingerprints

Add, delete, and rename fingerprints.

- In Settings, tap Biometrics & Security> Fingerprints for the following options:
  - ✓ The list of stored fingerprints is at the top of this list. You can press the fingerprint to erase or rename it.
  - ✓ Add a fingerprint: simply follow the instructions to register another fingerprint.
  - ✓ Verify that fingerprints are added: Scan the fingerprint to make sure it is registered.

Fingerprint Verification Settings

Verify your identity in supported applications and actions by identifying fingerprints.

- In Settings, tap Biometrics & Security> Fingerprints.
- ❖ Fingerprint unlock: Identify your fingerprint when you unlock the device.
- ❖ Fingerprint is always on: Scan your fingerprint even when the screen is off.
- ❖ Show icon when the screen is off: Displays the fingerprint icon when the screen is off.
- ❖ Show Unlock Animation: Displays the animation when using fingerprint verification.
- ❖ About unlocking with biometrics: Read details about the requirements that each biometric security feature has for using a pattern, PIN, or password as a backup.

Biometric Settings

Configure settings for biometric security options.

- In Settings, tap Biometrics & security> Advanced biometrics settings for the following:

- **Show gateway unlock effect:** Displays the gateway effect when you unlock your device with biometrics.
- **Biometric Security Correction:** View the software version of the biometric security features.

CHAPTER FIVE

DARK MODE

Dark mode allows you to switch to a darker theme to make your eyes more comfortable at night, dimming white or bright screens and notifications.

⊙ In the settings, tap Display for the following options:

l Light: Use a light color theme (default) on the device.

l Dark: Use a dark device on the device.

l Dark mode settings: Adjust when and where the dark mode is used.

- Turn on according to schedule: Configure dark sunset in sunrise mode or custom schedule.

Screen Brightness

Adjust the brightness of the screen according to lighting conditions or personal preferences.

1. In the settings, tap Display.

2. Adjust the options under Brightness:

- Drag the Brightness slider to adjust the custom brightness level.

- Touch Adjustable Brightness to automatically adjust the brightness of the screen according to the lighting conditions.

TIP You can also adjust the screen brightness in the Quick Settings panel.

Motion Smoothness

Enable smooth scrolling and more realistic animations by increasing the screen refresh rate.

1. In the settings, tap the screen> smoothness.

2. Touch, then tap Apply.

Eye Comfort Protector

The Eye Comfort Protector feature can help you sleep better and reduce eye strain.

You can set a schedule to turn this feature on and off automatically.

In Settings, tap Display> Eye Protection and select one of the following options:

- Touch to enable this feature.
- Touch Custom to automatically adjust the screen color temperature according to your usage patterns and time of day.
- Touch Custom to set a schedule when you need to enable eye protection.

- Touch Set Schedule and select Always On, Sunset to Sunrise, or Custom.

- Pull the temperature slider to adjust the opacity of the filter.

Display Mode

Your device has several display mode options that adapt the screen quality to different situations.

You can choose the mode to your liking.

1. In Settings, tap Display> Display Mode.

2. Touch to set another screen mode.

Font Size and Style

You can adjust the font size and style by customizing your device.

In Settings, tap Display> Font size and style for the following options:

> Press Font style to select another font.
> Tap a font to select it, or tap Download font to add fonts from the Galaxy Store.
> Touch bold to make all fonts bold.
> Drag the Font Size slider to adjust the text size.

Screen Magnification

Adjust the magnification level to make the content easier to see.

1. In Settings, tap Display> Zoom.

2. Drag the screen zoom slider to change the zoom level.

Screen Resolution

You can reduce the screen resolution to save battery power, or increase it to sharpen the image quality (Galaxy S21 Ultra 5G only).

1. In Settings, tap Display> Screen Resolution.

2. Touch the desired resolution and tap Apply.

NOTE Some programs may not support higher or lower screen resolution settings and may change when you change the resolution.

Full-Screen Applications

You can select which applications you want to use in full-screen mode.

○ In Settings, click Screen> Fullscreen and click apps to enable this feature.

Screen Operation

You can set the screen to turn off after a certain time.

> ➢ In Settings, tap Display> Screen timeout and tap Timeout to set it.

NOTE Prolonged display of still images, other than those always displayed, may result in permanent images such as a ghost or poor image quality.

Protect Against Accidental Touch

Prevent the screen from recognizing click input when the phone is in a dark place, such as a pocket or bag.

In Settings, tap Display> Random Touch Protection to enable the feature.

Touch sensitivity

Increase the touch alertness of the screen for use with screen protectors.

In Settings, tap Display> Touch Sensitivity to enable it.

Displaying Charging Information

When the display is off, the battery charge level and the estimated time until the device is fully charged can be displayed.

> In Settings, tap Display> Show information to enable them.

Screen saver

You can show colors or photos when the screen switches off or when charging it.

1. In Settings, tap Display> Screen saver.

2. Select one of the following options:

None: The screen saver is not displayed.

Colors: Touch the selector to display the screen that is changing.

> Photo table: display images in a photo table.
> Photo frame: display images in the photo frame.
> Photos: View images in your Google Photos account.

3. Touch Preview to display the selected screen saver.

TIP Tap Settings next to Advanced.

Lift to Wake Up

Turn on the display by lifting the device.

o In Settings, tap Advanced features> Gestures and gestures> Wake up to enable this feature.

Double-tap to turn on the screen.

To turn on the screen, double-tap instead of the side key.

- In Settings, tap Advanced features> Gestures & gestures> Double-tap to turn on the screen to enable this feature.

Double-tap to turn off the screen.

To turn off the screen, double-tap instead of the side key.

o In Settings, tap Advanced Features> Gestures & Gestures> Double-tap to turn off the screen to enable this feature.

Keep the screen on while watching.

Detect the front camera when you look at the screen to turn it on.

- In Settings, tap Advanced Features> Gestures & Gestures> Keep the screen on while watching, then tap to enable the feature.

One-handed mode

You can change the appearance of the screen to operate the device with one hand.

1. In Settings, tap Advanced Features> One Way Mode.

2. Touch to enable the feature, and select one of the following options:

- Move: drag down the middle of the bottom edge of the screen.
- Button: Double-tap Home to reduce the screen size.

CHAPTER SIX

GETTING STARTED
DEVICE LAYOUT (S21 5G)

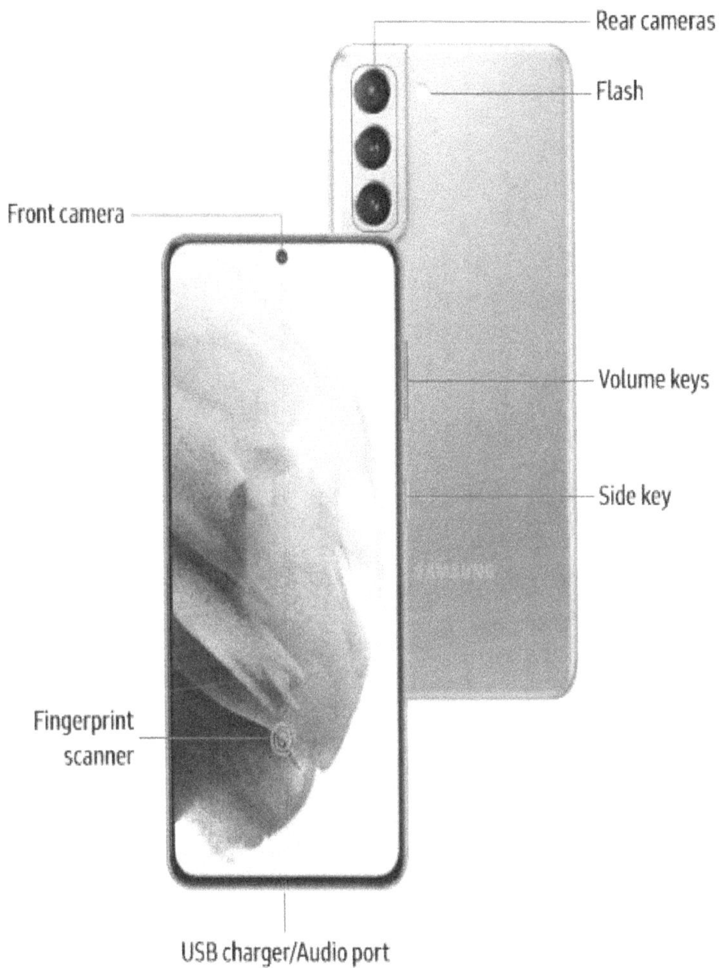

DEVICE LAYOUT (S21+ 5G)

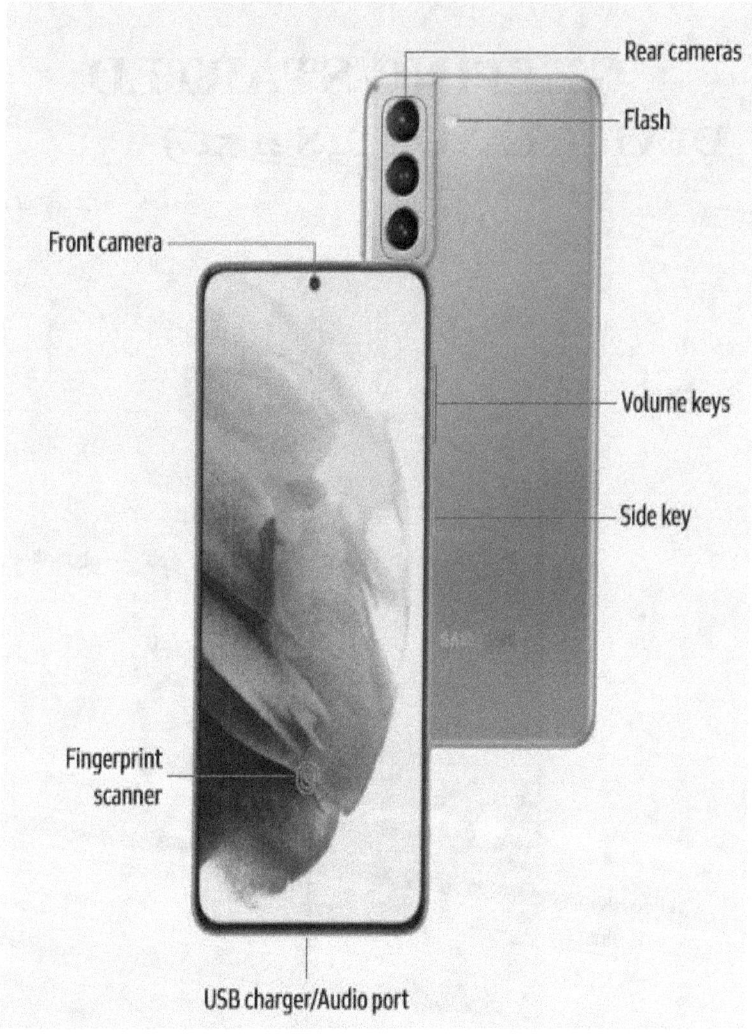

DEVICE LAYOUT (S21 ULTRA 5G)

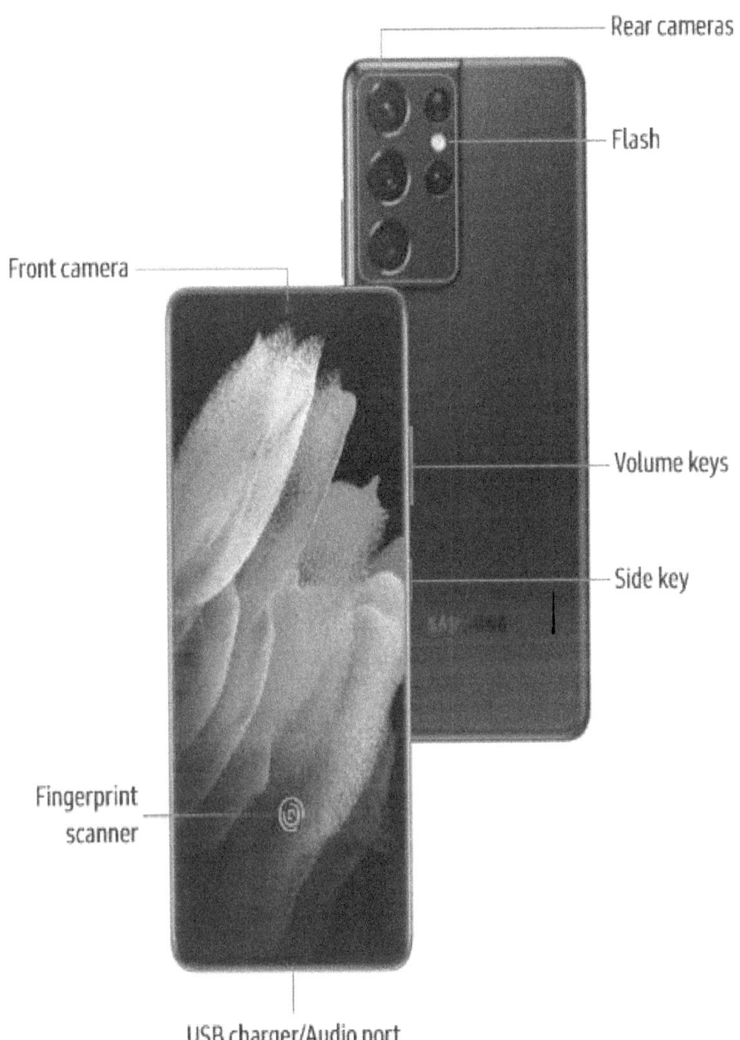

Set Up Your Device

Your device uses a nano-SIM card. The SIM card may be preinstalled, or you may be able to use your previous SIM card.

Nano-Sim Card and eSim

Insert the SIM or USIM card of your mobile service provider.

To have two phone numbers or a service provider for one device, activate eSIM or insert two SIM cards. Unlike a physical nano-SIM card, eSIM has a built-in digital SIM.

Using a nano-SIM and eSIM card may result in lower data rates in some areas.

- ✓ eSIM may not be available depending on your region, service provider, or model.
- ✓ Some services that require a network connection may not be available depending on your service provider.

Installing a SIM or USIM card

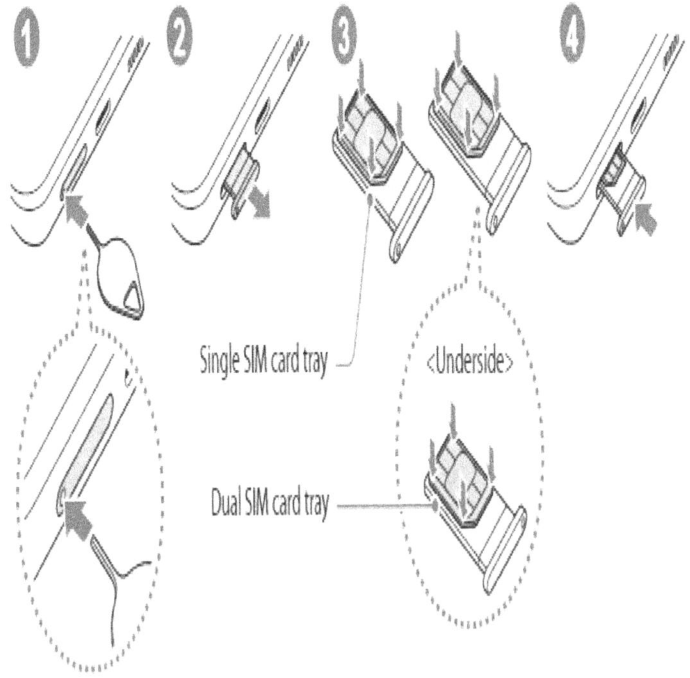

1 Insert the ejection needle into the hole in the tray to release the tray.

2 Gently pull the tray out of the slot.

3 Insert the SIM or USIM card into the tray with the gold-colored contacts facing up and gently push the SIM or USIM card into the tray to secure it.

4 Push in the tray into the slot.

- Insert the ejection needle into the tray opening to remove the tray.

Use only a nano-SIM card.

- Be careful not to lose or allow others to use your SIM or USIM card.
- Make sure that the eject pin is perpendicular to the opening. Otherwise, the device may be damaged.
- If the card is not firmly seated in the tray, the SIM card may leak or fall out of the tray.
- If you insert the tray into the device while the tray is wet, the device may be damaged. Always make sure the drawer is dry. Insert the tray completely into the slot to prevent liquid from entering the machine.

Activate eSIM

Launch the Settings application and tap Connections → SIM manager → Add mobile package. Once you find the mobile package, follow the on-screen instructions to activate eSIM.

If you have a QR code service provider, launch the Settings application, tap Connections → SIM card manager → Add mobile plan → Scan the QR operator code, and then scan the QR code.

SIM manager (dual SIM models)

Launch the Settings application and tap Connections → SIM manager.

- ✓ SIM cards: Activate the SIM card to use and adjust the SIM card settings.
- ✓ eSIM: activate eSIM.
- ✓ Preferred SIM card: Select to use some SIM cards for some functions, such as voice calls when two cards are activated.
- ✓ More SIM settings: adjust the call or eSIM settings.

Note The wall charger is sold separately; Use only Samsung-approved chargers and cables.

To reduce the risk of injury or damage to the device, do not use incompatible, worn, or damaged batteries, chargers, or cables.

The use of other chargers and batteries may void the warranty and cause damage.

Note Your IP68 device is dust and water-resistant. To maintain the device features that are resistant to water and dust, ensure that the openings on the SIM card tray are free of dust and water

Charging the battery

The device is powered by a rechargeable battery. A compatible USB Type-C cable is added to the Phone.

The USB Type-C cable can use a USB Type-C travel adapter, portable chargers, smartphones, laptops, wireless chargers, and other devices that offer USB-C ports for charging and transferring data.

Tip During charging, the device, and the charger may heat up and stop charging.

This usually does not affect the life or operation of the device and is within the normal range of the device.

Disconnect the charger from the device, and allow the device to cool

Wireless Power Sharing

Wirelessly charge compatible Samsung devices with your phone. Some functions are not available during power-sharing.

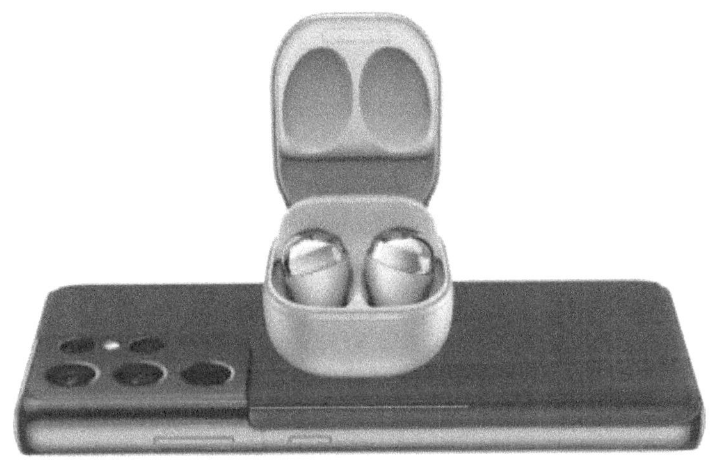

S-Sharing

1. In Settings, tap Battery and device care> Battery> Wireless power-sharing.

2. Touch Battery Limit and select a percentage.

When the charger reaches this charge level, wireless power-sharing is automatically turned off.

3. Touch to turn on the charging function.

4. To charge the phone, place the compatible device on the back of the phone. When charging starts, a notification sound or vibration sounds.

Keep in mind that Wireless power-sharing works with Qi-certified devices. You need about 30% battery to share.

Charging speed and energy efficiency vary by device. It may not work with some third-party accessories, covers, or devices.

If you have connection problems or the charging is slow, remove each cover from each device.

For best results when using wireless power-sharing, note the following:

- Erase any accessories or covers before using the feature. Depending on the kind of accessory or cover, wireless power-sharing may not function effectively.
- The position of the wireless charging coil may differ depending on the device, so you may need to adjust the position to establish a connection. When charging starts, a notification or vibration is displayed to allow you to connect.
- This may harper calls or data services, depending on the network.

+ Charging speed or efficiency may vary depending on the condition of the device or the environment.
+ Do not use the headset while charging with wireless split power.

Now Start to Use Your Device

Switching on the device

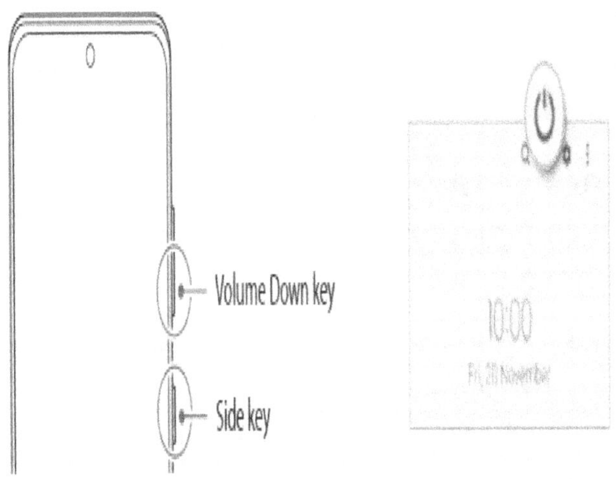

Switch on the device with the side key. Do not use the Phone if the body is cracked. Use it only after repair.

-Press and hold the side key to turn on the device.

o To turn off your device, press and hold the side and mute keys at the same time, and tap Turn off. Confirm when prompted.

- To restart the device, press and hold the side keys and the volume keys at the same time, then touch Restart. Confirm when prompted.

Forced Restart

If the phone is frozen and unresponsive, click and hold the side key and the Volume key down at once for more than 7 seconds to restart it.

Emergency Mode

You can switch the device to emergency mode to shorten battery usage.

Some applications and features will be limited. In an emergency, you can make an emergency call, send your current location information to others, trigger an emergency alarm, and more.

To activate emergency mode, press and hold the side key and the mute key at the same time, and then tap Emergency mode.

Or, open the notifications pane, drag down, and tap → Ambulance mode.

To turn off emergency mode, press → Turn off emergency mode.

The remaining usage time shows the remaining time before discharging the battery. The remaining usage time may vary depending on device settings and operating conditions

Using the Setup Wizard

When you turn on your device for the first time, the wizard guides you through the basics of setting up your device.

Follow the instructions to select your default language, connect to a Wi-Fi network, set up an account, select location services, learn about device features, and more.

Transfer Data from Your Old Device

With the smart switch, you can move contacts, photos, music, messages, notes, and more from your old device.

The Smart Switch can transfer your data via USB, Wi-Fi or PC.

1. In Settings, tap Accounts & Backups> Get Data from Old Device.

2. Follow the instructions and select the content to download.

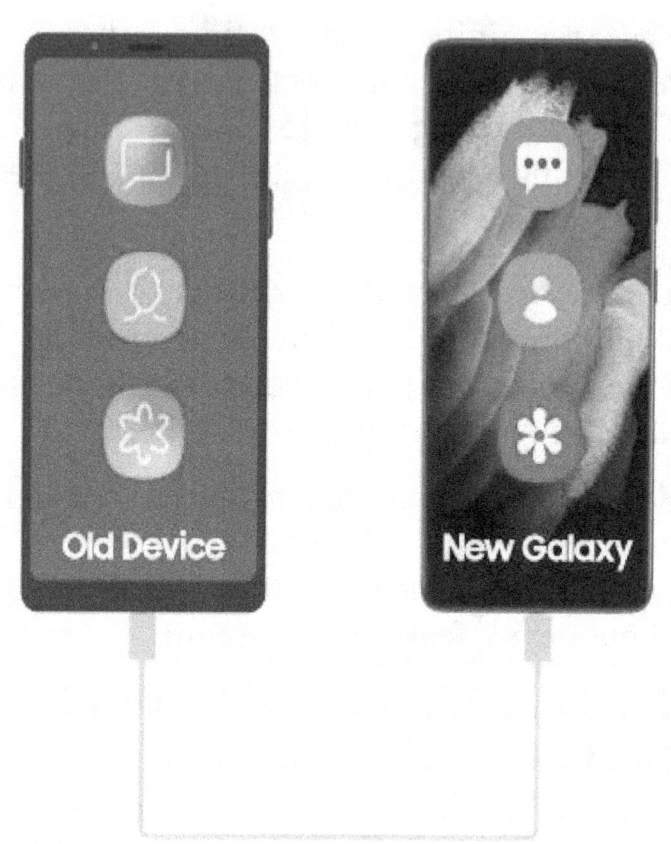

50

Lock or Unlock Your Device

Use the device lock features to protect your device. By default, the device locks automatically when the screen expires.

Side Key Settings

You can customize shortcuts to the side key.

Press twice

Select which function will be triggered when the side key is pressed twice.

51

1. In Settings, tap Advanced Features> Side Button.

2. Touch Double-click to enable this feature, then tap:

- Quick Launch Camera (default)

- Open Bixby

- Open the app

 Press and hold

Select which feature launches when you press and hold the side key.

1. In Settings, tap Advanced Features> Side Button.

2. Under the heading Press and hold, tap:

- Wake Bixby (default)

-shutdown menu

Account

Set up and manage your accounts.

Tip: Accounts can support email, calendars, contacts, and other features.

Add a Google Account

Sign in to your Google Account to access Google Cloud Storage, apps installed from your account, and take full advantage of Android device features.

1. In Settings, tap Accounts & Backups> Manage Accounts.

2. Touch Add Account> Google.

Add A Samsung Account

Log in to your Samsung account to access exclusive Samsung content and take full advantage of Samsung applications.

○ Touch Samsung account in the settings.

Add an Outlook account

Log in to your Outlook account to view and manage e-mail messages.

1. In Settings, tap Accounts & Backups> Manage Accounts.

2. Touch Add Account> Outlook.

Setting Up Voicemail

You can set up a voicemail when you access it for the first time. You can access your voicemail through the Phone app. Options vary by operator.

1. In your phone, tap and hold 1, or tap Voicemail.

2. Follow the instructions to create a password, record a greeting, and record a name.

Navigation

The touch screen responds best to a light touch of a finger pad or capacitive pen.

The use of excessive force or metal objects on the touch screen may damage the surface of the screen and the warranty is not covered by the warranty.

Touch items to select or launch them.

- Touch an item to select it.

- Twice click the image to enlarge or reduce it.

Slide

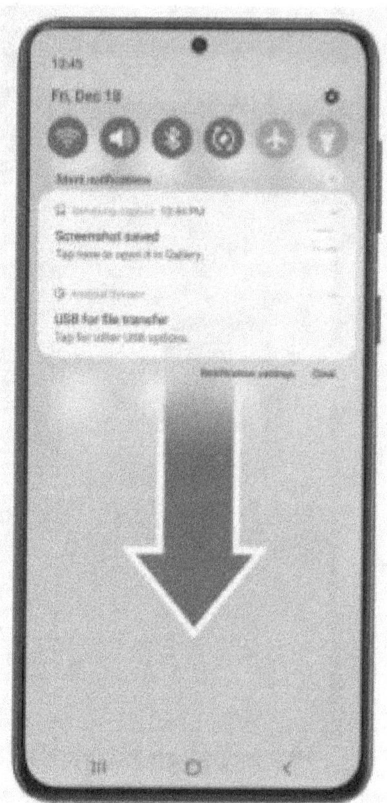

Gently slide your finger across the screen.

- Drag the screen to unlock the device.

- Drag the screen to scroll between the home screens or menu options.

Drag and drop

Touch and hold an item, then move it to a new location.

- Drag the application shortcut to add it to the Home screen.

- Drag the utility to set it in a new location.

Touch and hold

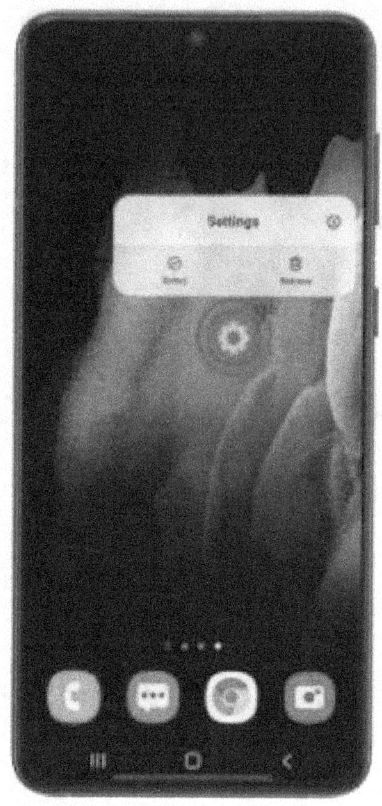

Touch and hold items to activate them.

-Touch and hold a field to display a pop-up menu with options.

-Touch and hold the Home screen to adjust the Home screen.

UNDERSTAND YOUR SCREEN

Controlling the touch screen

1.Tapping Tap the screen.

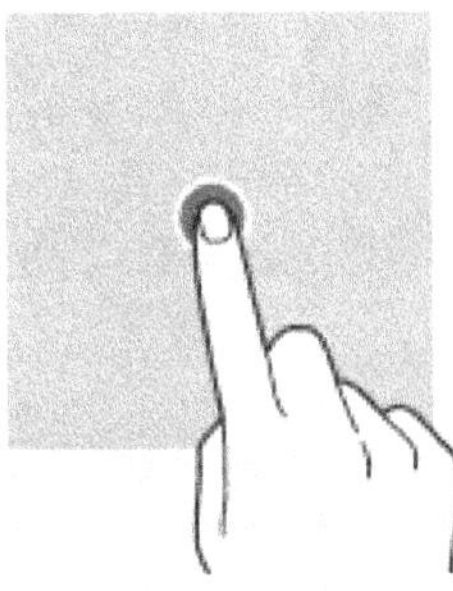

2.Tap and hold Tap and hold the screen for about 2 seconds.

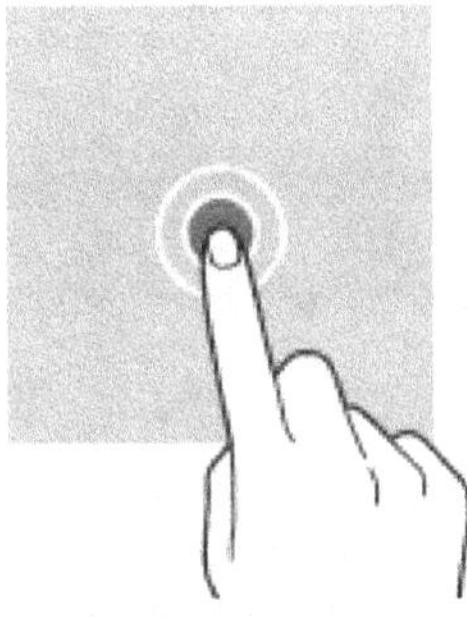

3.Drag Touch and hold an item and drag it to the destination.

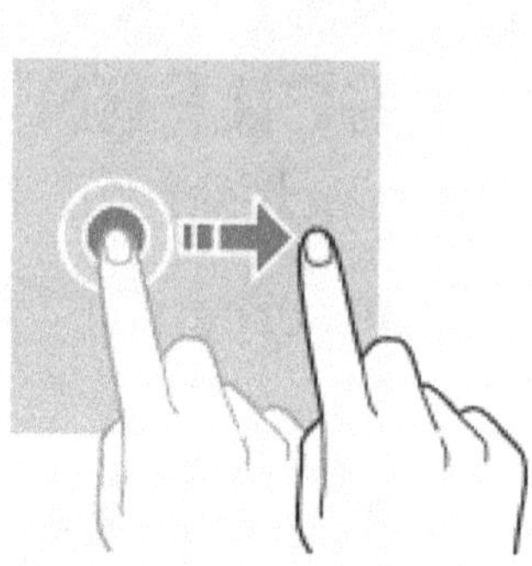

4.Double-tap Double-tap the screen.

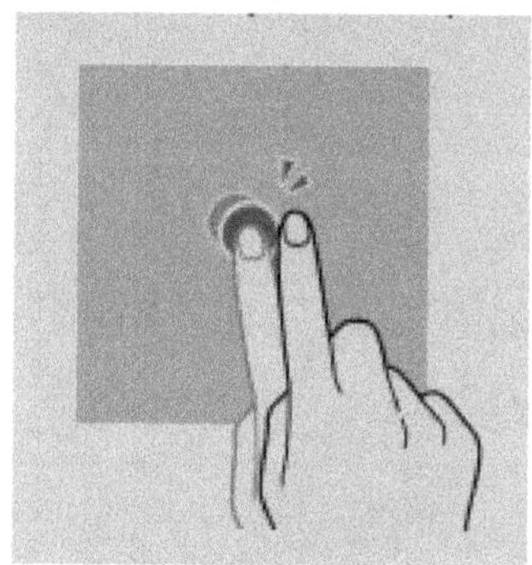

5.Drag Drag up, down, left, or right.

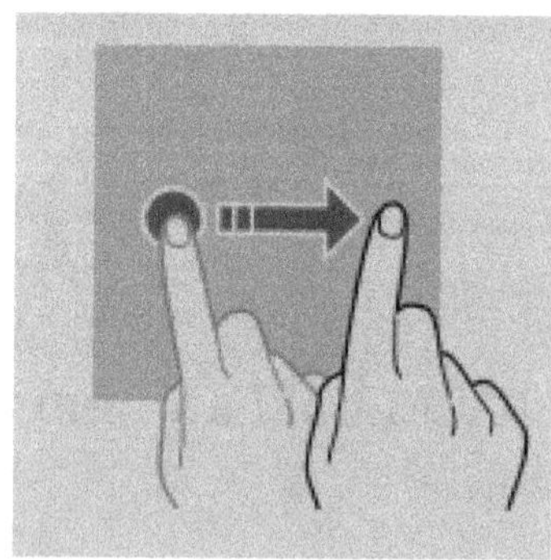

6.Expand and squeeze Spread two fingers or squeeze the screen.

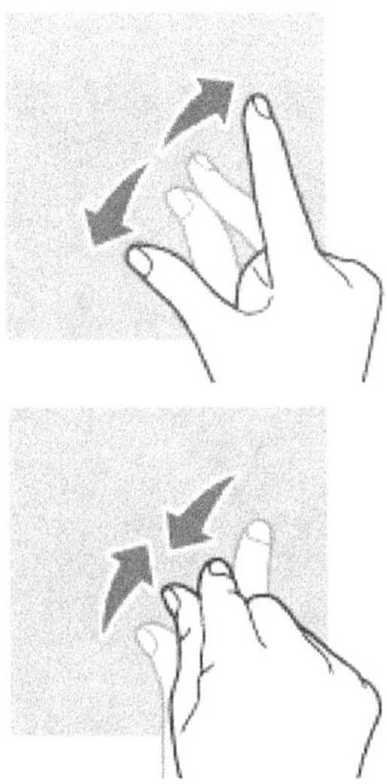

  ✓ Make sure the touch screen does not
    come into contact with other electrical
    devices. Electrostatic discharges can
    damage the touch screen.
  ✓ To avoid damaging the touch screen, do
    not tap it with sharp touches or press it
    with your fingertips.
  ✓ It is recommended that you do not use
    fixed graphics on part of the touch
    screen or in full screen for an extended
    time.

This can cause further images (screen burn) or ghosts.

NAVIGATION BAR

You can move the device with the navigation buttons or gestures in full-screen mode.

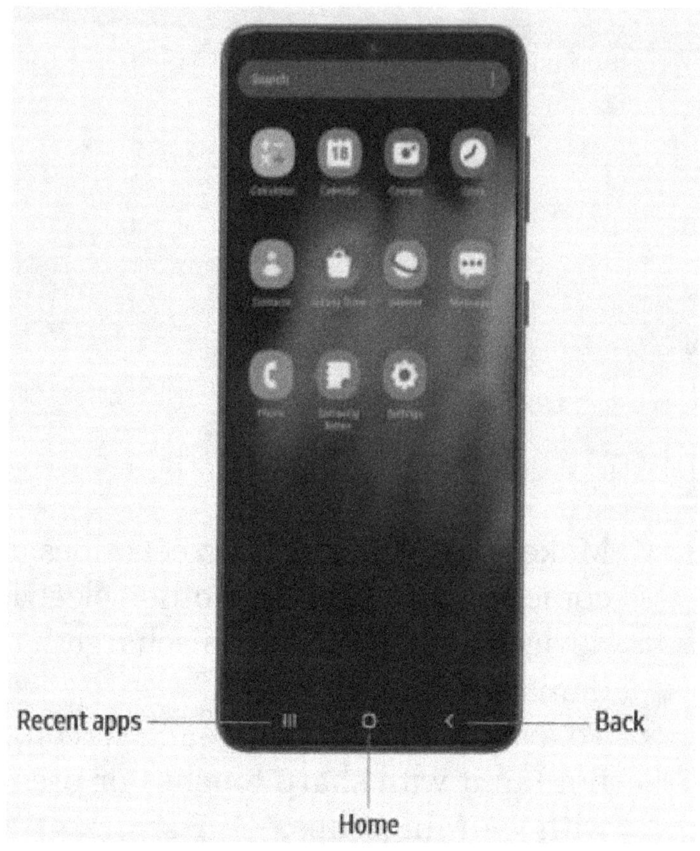

Navigation Buttons

Use the buttons at the bottom of the screen to navigate quickly.

1. In Settings, tap Display> Navigation bar> Buttons.

2. Touch the option below the button to select which side of the screen the Back and Recent Applications icons appear.

Navigation Gestures

Hide the navigation buttons at the bottom of the screen for a smooth screen experience. Instead, drag to navigate the device.

1. In Settings, tap Display> Navigation bar> Finger gestures to enable the feature.

2. Touch customization options:

- More options: select a stroke type and sensitivity.

- Tips for gestures: Display the lines at the bottom of the screen where each move of the screen is.

- Show button to hide the keyboard: Show the icon in the lower right corner of the screen to hide the keyboard when the device is in portrait mode.

- Blocking strokes with the S stylus: Prevent the S stylus from performing navigation strokes (Galaxy S21 Ultra 5G only).

Personalize Your Home Screen

The home screen is your starting point for navigating your device. Here you can place your favorite apps and gadgets

and set up additional home screens, remove screens, change the screen order, and select the main home screen.

Application Icons

Use application icons to launch an application from any Home screen.

○ In apps, tap and hold the app icon, then tap Add to the homepage. To remove an icon:

○ From the Home screen, touch and hold the app icon, then tap Remove.

NOTE Removing the application icon will not delete it, but only from the Home screen.

Wallpaper

Change the look of your home and lock the screen by selecting your favourite picture, video, or preloaded wallpaper.

1. From the Home screen, touch and hold the screen, then tap Wallpapers.

2. Touch one of the following menus for available wallpapers:

• My wallpapers: Choose from highlighted and downloaded wallpapers.

• Gallery: Select images and videos stored in the gallery.

• Wallpaper services: Enable additional features, including a guide page and a Dynamic Lock screen.

• Use dark background mode: enable dark background mode.

• Explore multiple wallpapers: Find and download multiple wallpapers from Galaxy Themes.

3. Touch an image or video to select it.

• If you select one image, select the screen or screens on which you want to apply the background.

• You can use videos and multiple pictures only on the lock screen.

• To select videos or images from Gallery, tap one or more items, and then tap Done.

4. Touch Home screen settings, Lock screen settings, or Lock and home screen settings (depending on which screens apply).

• If you use the wallpaper on the Home and Lock screens, enable Sync My Changes if you want the edits on that wallpaper to apply to both screens.

Themes

Set the theme that you want to use on the home and lock screens, wallpapers, and application icons.

1. From the Home screen, press and drag the screen.

2. Tap Themes and tap a theme to view and download it.

3. Tap the navigation tray> My stuff> Themes to view the downloaded themes.

4. Touch a theme, then tap Apply to use the selected theme.

Icons

Use different sets of icons to override the default icons.

1. From the Home screen, click and hold the screen.

2. Tap Themes> Icons, and then tap the icon set to view and download.

3. Tap the navigation tray> My stuff> Icons to view the downloaded icons.

4. Tap the icon, then tap Apply to use the selected icon set

Gadgets

Add gadgets to your home screens for quick access to information or applications.

1. From the Home screen, click and hold the screen.

2. Touch gadgets, then tap the gadget you want to open.

3. Drag to the gadget you want to add to the Home screen, then tap Add.

Customize a widget

When you add a widget, you can customize where it is located and how it works.

○ From the Home screen, press and drag a gadget, and then click:

• Remove: Delete the gadget from the screen.

• Settings: customize the function or appearance of the gadget.

• Application information: see gadget usage, permissions, and more.

Home Screen Settings

Customize your home screen and app screens.

1. From the Home screen, press and drag the screen.

2. Touch Settings to customize:

Home screen layout: Set your device to have a separate home screen and app screens, or just a home screen that has all the apps.

Home screen grid: Select a layout to define the layout of the icons on the Home screen.

Application screen grid: Select a layout to specify the layout of the icons on the application screen.

> ➢ Home Apps Screen button: Add a button to the Home screen for easy access to the Apps screen.
> ➢ Lock Home screen layout: Prevent removing or moving items from the Home screen.
> ➢ Add new applications to the home screen: automatically add newly downloaded applications to the home screen.

- ➤ Hide apps: select the apps you want to hide from the Home screen and the Apps screen. Return to this screen to restore hidden programs. Hidden applications are still installed and can be displayed as results in the Finder.
- ➤ Application icon badges: Enable the display of badges in applications with active notifications. You can also select a badge style.
- ➤ Drag down for the notification pane: Enable this feature to open the notification pane by dragging anywhere on the Home screen.
- ➤ Rotate in landscape mode: rotates the home screen automatically when the orientation of the device changes from portrait to landscape.
- ➤ About home screen: display version information.

Easy Mode

Easy Mode contains larger text and icons for a simpler visual experience. Switch between the default screen layout and an easier layout.

1. In Settings, tap Display> Easy Mode.

2. Touch to enable this feature. These options are showed:

- ✓ Touch and hold delay: Set how much it takes for a regular touch to be recognized.
- ✓ High-contrast keyboard: Select a keyboard with high-contrast colors

Dashboard

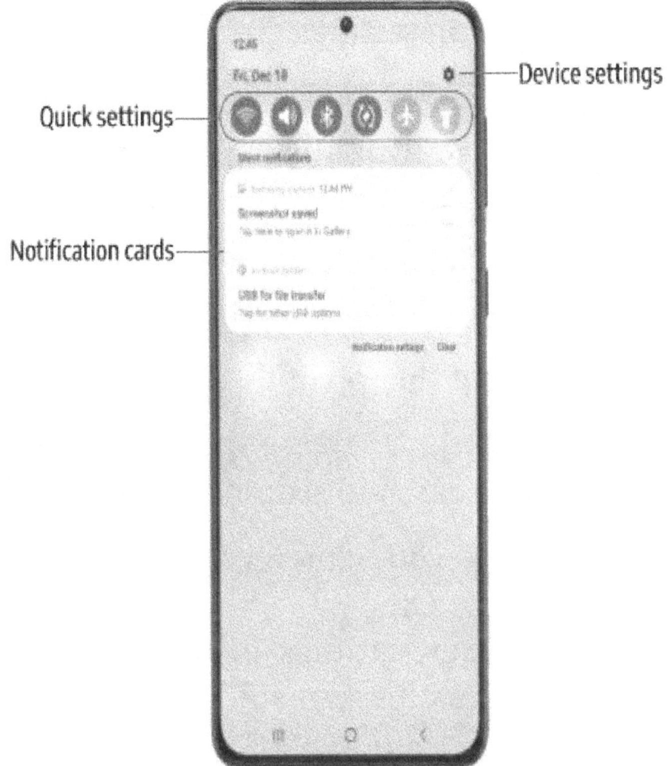

View the notification pane

You can access the notification pane from any screen.

1. Swipe down from the screen to display the notification panel.

• To open an item, tap it.

   ✓ To delete a notification, drag it left or right.

71

✓ To clear all notifications, tap Clear.
✓ To customize notifications, tap Notification settings.

2. Swipe up from the bottom of the screen, or tap Back to close the notification panel.

Quick Settings

The notification pane provides quick access to device features using quick settings.

Slide down from the top of the screen to show fast settings.

Touch Finder search to search for devices.

✓ To turn it off, emergency mode, and restart, tap Off.
✓ Touch Open settings to quickly access the device settings menu.
✓ Touch More options to rearrange quick settings or change the button layout.
✓ Touch Device to manage other devices when supported applications such as SmartThings or Google Home are installed.
✓ Tap Media to open the Media panel and control the playback of connected audio and video devices.

• Touch the quick setting icon to turn it on or off.

• Touch and hold the quick settings icon to open it.

View the notification panel

From the screen, notification panel can be accessed

1. Swipe down from the screen to display the notification panel.

• To open an item, tap it.

• To delete a notification, drag it left or right.

• To clear all notifications, tap Clear.

• To customize notifications, tap Notification settings.

2. Swipe up from the bottom of the screen, or tap Back to close the notification panel.

Quick settings

The notification pane provides quick access to device features using quick settings.

Slide down from the top of the screen to show fast settings.

• Touch Finder search to search for devices.

• To turn it off, emergency mode, and restart, tap Off.

• Touch Open settings to quickly access the device settings menu.

• Touch More options to rearrange quick settings or change the button layout.

• Touch Device to manage other devices when supported applications such as SmartThings or Google Home are installed.

• Tap Media to open the Media panel and control the playback of connected audio and video devices.

• Touch the quick setting icon to turn it on or off.

• Touch and hold the quick settings icon to open it.

CHAPTER SEVEN

MULTI WINDOW AND EDGE PANEL

Multitasking with multiple applications simultaneously. Edge applications that support multiple windows can be displayed together on a separate screen. You can switch between apps and resize them.

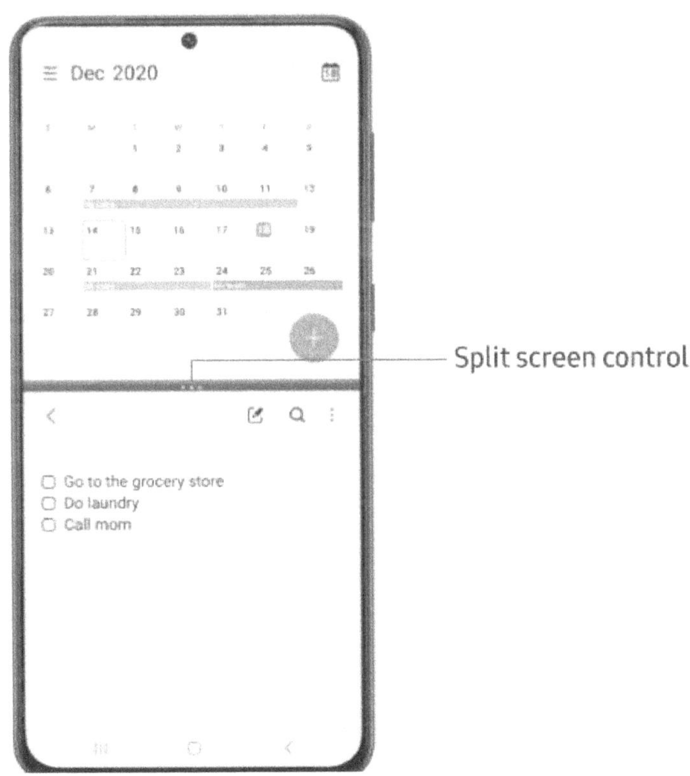

1. On any screen, tap the Latest apps.

2. Tap the app icon, then tap Open in a separate screen view.

3. Tap the app in another window to add it to the split-screen view.

• Drag the center of the window border to adjust the window size.

Window Controllers

Window Controllers change the way the application window is displayed in a separate screen view.

1. Drag the center of the window border to resize the window.

2. Touch the center of the window border for the following options:

• Change window: replace two windows.

• Add apps together to the Edge panel: Create and add a shortcut in pairs of apps to the panel on the side screen.

Edge Panel

The edges of the panel contain a series of customizable panels that can be accessed from the edge of the screen.

You can use Edgeboards to access apps, tasks, and contacts, and to view news, sports, and other information.

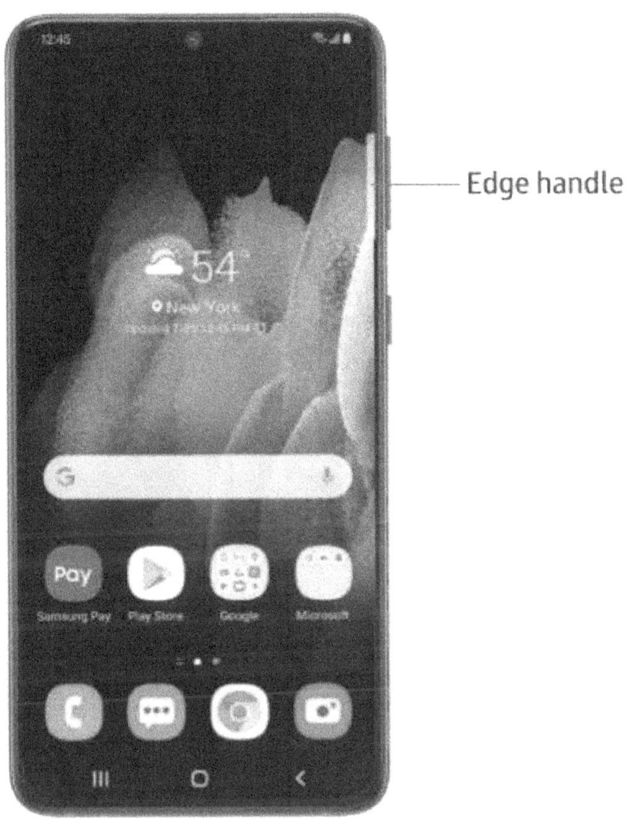

Application Panel

You can add programs in two columns to the application pane.

1. From any screen, drag the Edge lever to the center of the screen. Drag until the app's pane appears.

2. Tap an app or shortcut in a pair of apps to open it. You can also tap All apps for a full list of apps.

- To open additional windows in the pop-up view, drag the application icon from the Applications panel to the open screen.

To configure the application panel:

1. On any screen, drag the Edge lever to the center of the screen. Drag until the app's pane appears.

2. Touch Edit panel to add other programs to the application panel.

• To create a folder shortcut, drag an app to the left of the screen at the top of the app in the columns on the right.

• To change the order of the applications on the panel, drag each application to the desired location.

• To uninstall an app, tap Uninstall. 3. Touch Back to save the changes.

Configuring Edge panels

You can customize Edge panels.

1. On the Edge screen, tap Settings.

2. The following options are available:

• Check box: enable or disable each panel.

• Edit (if available): Configure individual panels.

• Search: Search for panels that are installed or available for installation.

• More options: - Rearrange: change the order of the panels by dragging left or right.

- Hide on lock screen: Select the panels you want to hide on the lock screen when the secure screen lock is set.

• Galaxy Store: Find and download multiple Edge discs from the Galaxy Store.

3. Touch Back to save the changes.

Edge Panel Position and Style

You can change the position of the edge edges.

○ In Settings, tap Display> Edge boards> Handle for the following options:

• Edge handle: Drag to change the position of the edge along the edge of the screen.

• Position: Select Right or Left to set which side the Edge screen will be displayed on.

• Lock position: Allow you to prevent the handle position from moving when you touch and hold it.

• Style: Select a color for the Edge handle.

• Transparency: Drag the slider to change the Edge handle.

• Size: Drag the slider to change the Edge handle.

About Edge Panels

You can view the current software version and license information for Edge Panels.

○ In Settings, tap Display> Edge boards> About Edges.

Enter Text

You can put text either with the keyboard or voice.

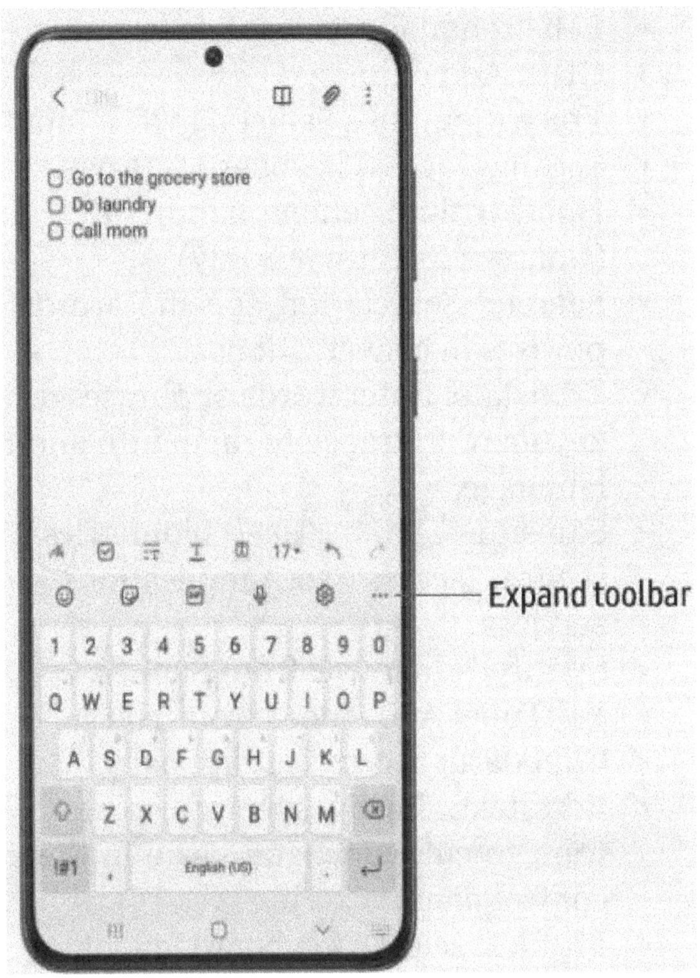

Toolbar

The toolbar provides quick access to keyboard functions. Options may vary by operator.

○ On the Samsung keyboard, tap Expand toolbar for the following options:

• Emoji's: Insert emoticons.

✓ Labels: add illustrated labels.
✓ GIFs: Add animated GIFs.
✓ Voice input: use Samsung voice input.
✓ Settings: access keyboard settings.
✓ Handwriting: enter handwritten text (Galaxy S21 Ultra 5G only).
✓ Search: Search for specific words or phrases in conversations.
✓ Translate: Enter words or phrases on the keyboard to translate them into another language.
✓ Samsung Pass: Use biometrics for secure access to applications and services.
✓ Spotify: add music from Spotify.
✓ YouTube: Add videos from YouTube.
✓ Clipboard: access the clipboard.
✓ Edit text: Easily specify the text you want to cut, copy, and paste in the edit control panel.
✓ Profiles: select a keyboard layout.
✓ Keyboard size: Adjust or increase the height and width of it.
✓ Bitmos: create your emojis and use them in stickers.
✓ AR emojis: create your emojis and use them in stickers that you can share.
✓ Mytok: create your labels or insert automatically suggested labels.

Configuring the Samsung keyboard

Set custom options for the Samsung keyboard.

○ On the Samsung keyboard, tap Settings for the following options:

• **Languages and types**: set the keyboard type and choose which languages will be available on the keyboard.

- To switch from one language to another, swipe left or right. Start typing

• **Predictive text**: View suggested words and phrases during playback.

• **Suggest emoji**: turn on emoji when using predictive text.

• **Suggest stickers as you type**: See recommended stickers as you type.

• **Auto-replace:** automatically replaces the text you enter with text prediction recommendations.

• **Automatic spell check:** Underline misspelled words in red and suggest corrections.

• **More typing options**: Customize additional typing options. Style and appearance

• **Keyboard toolbar**: Shows or hides the keyboard toolbar.

• **High-contrast keyboard**: Rearrange the keyboard and adjust its colors to improve the contrast between the keys and the background.

• **Theme**: select a theme for the keyboard.

• **Mode:** Select portrait or landscape mode.

• **Appearance**: Displays numbers and special characters on the keyboard.

• **Custom symbols:** Change shortcuts to symbols on the keyboard.

• Swipe, tap, and feedback with your finger: Adjust gestures and feedback.

• Handwriting: adjust handwriting options (Galaxy S21 Ultra 5G only).

• Select the third-party content you want to use: enable external keyboard features.

• Restore default settings: Restore the keyboard to its original settings and delete customer data.

• About the Samsung keyboard: See the version and legal information for the Samsung keyboard.

• Contact us: Contact Samsung support through Samsung members (if supported by your operator).

Use Samsung voice input

Enter text in speech instead of entering text.

○ On the Samsung keyboard, tap Voice input and speak the text.

Configuring Samsung voice input

Set custom options for Samsung voice input.

1. On the Samsung keyboard, tap Voice input.

2. Touch Settings.

• Keyboard language: Select a keyboard language.

• About Samsung voice input: See the version and legal information about Samsung voice input.

Emergency Mode

Use the emergency mode to access useful emergency functions and to save power to the emergency device.

To save battery power, emergency mode:

• Limit the use of applications to key applications and just select them.

• Turns off connection functions and mobile data when the screen is off.

Activate emergency mode

To activate emergency mode:

1. Press and hold the side keys and the volume keys at the same time.

2. Touch Solution Mode.

• When you access for the first time, read and accept the terms and conditions.

3. Touch On.

Emergency Mode Features

On the home screen, only the following applications and features are available in emergency mode. Options may vary by operator.

- Estimated battery life: Displays the estimated remaining battery charge time based on current battery charge and consumption.

- Flashlight: Use the flash of the device as a permanent light source.

- Emergency alarm: An audible siren sounds.

- Phone: Start the dialing screen.

- Share / Send my location: send your location information to emergency contacts.

- Internet: Launch a web browser.

- Chrome: Launch Google's web browser.

- Emergency call: Call the emergency number (for example, 911). You can also make such a call without activating the service.

- More options: - Deactivate emergency mode: Disable emergency mode and return to standard mode.

- Edit: add or remove Programs from the screen.

- Emergency contacts: manage your medical profile and ICE contacts (in emergencies).

- Settings: Only a few settings are enabled on emergency mode.

Deactivating Emergency Mode

When an emergency mode is deactivated, the device returns to standard mode.

Press more options and click switch off emergency mode.

CHAPTER EIGHT

CAMERA AND GALARY APP

You can take high-quality images and videos with the Camera application.

Pictures and videos are saved in Gallery, where you can view and edit them.

Camera

Enjoy a full range of professional lenses and professional video modes and settings.

◌ In the applications, tap Camera.

Tip If Quick Launch is enabled, press the side key twice quickly to open the Camera application.

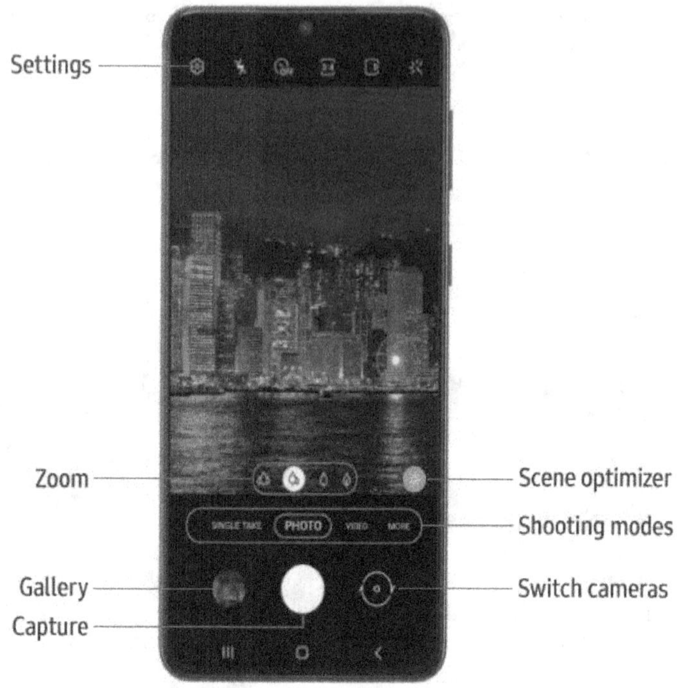

Scrolling the camera screen

Capture stunning images with the front and rear cameras of the device.

1. In the Camera application, set a shot with the following features:

• Click the screen to the position you want the camera to face.

- When you touch the screen, the brightness scale is displayed. Drag the light slider.

• To quickly switch between the front and rear cameras, swipe up or down on the screen.

• To switch to another shooting mode, swipe right or left on the screen.

• To adjust the camera settings, press settings.

2. Touch Record.

Configuring Shooting Mode

Allow the camera to determine the ideal mode for your images, or select one of several shooting modes.

In the camera, swipe right and left on the screen to change the shooting mode.

• Single shot: Take multiple pictures and videos from different angles.

• Photo: Allow the camera to set the ideal picture settings.

• Video: Allow the camera to set the ideal video settings.

• More: select other available shooting modes. Touch Add to drag mode to or from the shooting mode tray at the bottom of the camera screen.

AR Doodle: Enhance your videos by adding line drawings to the environment.

AR Doodle monitors faces and space so they move with you. - Pro: Manually adjust ISO sensitivity, exposure value, white balance, and color tone during shooting. - Panorama: Create a linear image by shooting horizontally or vertically. Food: Take pictures that highlight the vivid colors of the food.

- Night: Use this to take photos in low light without using the flash.

- Portrait: Adjust the background of the shots for portrait photos.

- Portrait video: Set the wallpaper for portrait videos.

- Pro video: Manually adjust ISO sensitivity, exposure value, white balance, and color tone during movie recording.

- Super slow motion: Record videos at extremely high frame rates for viewing in high-quality slow motion. After recording, you can play a slow-motion clip of a specific section of each video. -

 Slow-motion: Record videos at a high frame rate for slow-motion viewing.

- Hyper lapse: Create time-lapse videos by shooting at different frame rates.

The number of frames per second is adjusted according to the recorded scene and the movement of the device.

AR area

Access all augmented reality (AR) functions in one place.

○ In-Camera, drag to More, then tap the AR area. The following features are available:

- ✓ AR Emoji Camera: is used to create your Emoji avatar.
- ✓ AR Doodle: Enhance videos by adding line drawings or manuscripts to the environment. AR Doodle monitors faces and space so they move with you.
- ✓ AR Emoji Studio: create and customize your Emoji avatar.
- ✓ AR Emoji Stickers: is use add AR stickers to your Emoji avatar.
- ✓ Deco Pic: Decorate photos or videos with the camera in real-time.

Scene Optimizer

Automatically adjusts brightness, contrast, white balance, and more based on what is detected in the camera to help you take beautiful photos.

⊙ Drag from the camera to Photo and tap Scene optimizer.

NOTE The Scene Optimizer is only available when the rear camera is used. The scene optimizer icon will automatically change depending on what the camera recognizes, such as when taking pictures in nature or shooting in a dark environment.

One-Shot

Capture more in each frame, and take photos and videos at the same time. This mode of photography uses artificial intelligence to create high-quality images and videos from multiple angles. The number of pictures and videos may vary.

1. Slide your finger from the camera to the shot.

2. Tap 10s and select a timer option.

3. Touch Capture and scroll the scene to capture more angles and views. Videos and pictures will be saved as one entry in the gallery.

Zoom Range

Shoot up to 100x magnification with clarity and accuracy (zoom options may vary by model).

1. In the camera, touch the zoom shortcut to select the zoom setting.

• When shooting at a higher magnification, point the target at the frame and touch Zoom to zoom quickly and accurately (Galaxy S21 Ultra 5G only).

2. Touch Record.

Capture Videos

Capture smooth actual videos with your device.

1. In the Camera, swipe right or left to change the recording mode to Video.

2. Touch Record to start recording the video.

• To take a photo while taking a photo, tap Capture.

• To stop recording, tap Pause. To resume recording, tap Continue.

3. When you have finished recording, touch Stop.

Director's View

Create videos with seamless transitions between multiple camera angles. Dual shot from the front and rear camera and allows multiple shots with Picture-in-picture or Split screen.

1. From the Camera, drag to More, then tap Director View.

2. Touch View Type to switch between single view, picture-in-picture, and split view.

3. Touch Record.

-Aim the camera at the subject and tap one of the available lens replacement windows.

- Touch if the windows are not visible.

- Swipe up or down the screen to switch between the front and rear cameras.

4. When you have finished recording, touch Stop.

Increase the Microphone

Increase the volume of the recorded sound and reduce the background noise when you increase the sound source in Video mode. This function cannot be used with other video modes or the front camera.

1. In-Camera, tap Settings.

2. Touch Advanced Recording Options> Enlarge Microphone and tap to enable.

3. Touch Back to return to the main camera screen.

4. Drag to change the recording mode to Video.

5. Touch Recording to start recording.

6. Connect or spread your fingers on the screen to increase or decrease the sound source. The microphone icon indicates the level of amplification used.

Camera Settings

Use the icons on the main camera screen and the settings menu to configure the camera settings.

◌ Touch Settings on the camera for the following options: Smart Features

• Scene Optimizer: Automatically adjust the color settings of the images to match the theme.

• Snapshot suggestions: Get on-screen guides to help you edit great shots.

• QR code scan: Automatically detect QR codes when using the camera. Pictures

• Drag the shutter button to: Select whether you want to take a sequence shot or create a GIF when you press the shutter button to the nearest edge.

• Format and advanced options: select file formats and other storage options.

- HEIF images: save images as high-performance images to save space.

- RAW copies: save JPEG and RAW copies of images taken in Pro mode.

- Exceptional shape correction: automatically corrects distortion in images taken with an ultra-wide lens.

Selfies

• Use wide-angle group selfies: Automatically switch to wide-angle when two or more people are in self-portraits.

• Save self-portraits in the preview: save the self-portraits as shown in the preview without tipping over.

• Self-portrait color tone: Set the color tone for your selfie to Natural or Bright.

Videos

- High-performance videos: Record videos in HEVC format to save space. Other sharing devices or websites may not support the playback of this format.

- HDR10 + videos: Optimize videos by recording in HDR10 +. Playback devices must support HDR10 + video.

- Microphone magnification: When recording a video, connect the microphone magnification to the camera magnification.

• Video Stabilization: Activate anti-shake to keep the sharpness stable while moving the camera.

Useful features

• Auto HDR: Capture more detail in light and dark areas of images.

• Autofocus tracking: keep the moving subject in focus.

• Gridlines: See the gridlines of the viewfinder to help you compose an image or video.

• Location markers: Attach a GPS location marker to images and videos.

- Voice commands: take photos by saying keywords.

- Floating shutter-release button: Add shutter-release button that can be moved anywhere on the screen.

- Show palm: extend your hand with the palm facing the camera to take a photo within seconds.

• Hold settings: Select whether the camera starts with the same shooting mode, selfie angle, and filters as last time.

• Shutter sound: Play a tone while recording.

• Vibrating feedback: Enable vibrating when you tap the screen in the Camera app.

• Reset settings: Reset the camera settings.

• Contact us: Contact Samsung support through Samsung members (if supported by your operator).

• About camera: View information about the application and software.

DIRECTOR'S VIEW MODE

Shoot videos from different angles by changing the camera. In this mode, the subject and the person can be recorded at the same time.

1 In the list of shooting modes, press More - Director View.

2 Select the desired camera screen and thumbnail, then tap to record a video.

• To change the screen before recording, tap and select the desired screen.

• You can change the camera thumbnail during recording. If the thumbnail is hidden, tap to show it.

3 Touch to stop recording videos.

GALLERY

Go to Gallery to see all the visual media stored on your device. You can view, edit and manage your images and videos.

○ Tap Gallery between apps.

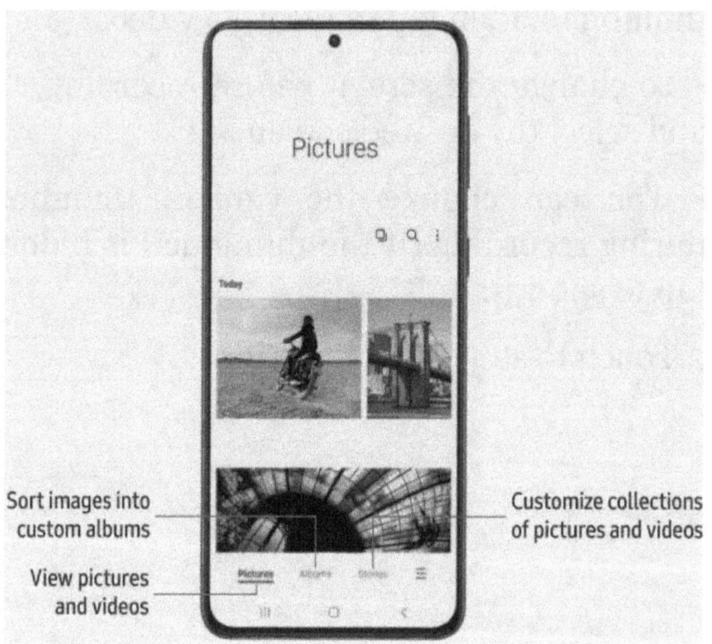

View Images

You can view images stored on your device in Gallery.

1. In the gallery, tap Pictures.

2. Touch the image to view it. Slide left or right to look at other pictures or videos.

• To use Bixby Vision in the current image, tap Bixby Vision. See Bixby for more information.

• To mark a picture as a favorite, click Add to favorites.

• To access these features, press more options:

- Details: View and edit image information.

- Copy to clipboard: Copy the image to paste it into another application.

- Move to secure folder: Move the image to a secure folder.

- Print: Send the image to a connected printer.

Edit Pictures

Enhance your pictures with the gallery editing tool.

1. In the gallery, tap Pictures.

2. Touch an image to view it, and then touch Edit for the following options:

• Format: Rotate, rotate, crop, or change the entire image.

• Filters: add color effects.

• Tone: adjust brightness, brightness, contrast, and more.

• Labels: Overlay illustrated or animated labels.

• Text: add text to the image.

• Portrait: enhances skin tones, eyes, and other facial features.

• Auto Adjustment: Use Auto Adjustment to enhance the image.

• Restore: Undo changes to restore the original image.

3. When you are finished, touch Save.

Play A Video

View videos stored on your device. You can save videos as favorites and view details about them.

1. In the gallery, tap Pictures.

2. Press a video to watch it.

• To mark a video as a favorite, click Add to favorites. The video has been added to Favorites on the Albums tab.

• To access these features, press more options:

- Details: View and edit video information.

- Set as wallpaper: set a wallpaper video on the lock screen.

- Move to Safe Folder: Add this video to your Safe Folder.

3. Touch Play Video to play the video.

Video Enhancer

1. In Settings, tap Advanced Features> Video Enhancer.

2. Touch to enable this feature.

Edit Videos

Edit videos stored on your device.

1. In the gallery, tap Pictures.

2. Touch a video to watch it.

3. Touch Edit to use the following tools:

• Play: Watch the edited video.

• Crop: cut video segments.

• Transform: Rotate, rotate, crop, or change the overall look of the video.

• Label: Overlay illustrated or animated labels.

• Draw: draw a video.

• Text: Add text to videos.

• Portrait: enhances skin tones, eyes, and other facial features.

• Speed: Adjust the playback speed.

• Sound: Adjust the volume and add background music to the video.

4. Touch Save, and then confirm when prompted.

Share Pictures and Videos

Share pictures and videos from the gallery.

1. In the gallery, tap Pictures.

2. Touch More Options> Edit and select the pictures or videos you want to share.

3. Touch Sharing, and then select the application or connection you want to share with others. Follow the instructions.

Delete Pictures and Videos

Erase pictures and videos saved on the phone.

1. In the gallery, tap More options> Edit.

2. Touch pictures and videos to select them.

3. Touch Delete and confirm when prompted.

Combine Similar Images

Sort images and videos in the gallery by similarity.

1. In the gallery, tap Similar image groups.

2. Touch Dissolve Similar Images to return to the default Gallery view.

Take a screenshot.

The device will automatically create a screenshot album in the gallery.

On any screen, press and release the side keys and the volume down keys.

Drag to Take a Screenshot

Take a screenshot by dragging the edge of your hand from one side to the other to keep in touch with the screen.

1. In Settings, tap Advanced Features> Gestures & Gestures> Drag to capture.

2. Touch to enable this feature.

Screenshot Settings
Change the screenshot settings.

○ In Settings, tap Advanced Features> Screenshots and Screensaver.

- Screen toolbar: Displays additional options after taking a screenshot.

-Hide status bars and navigation bars: Do not show status bars or navigation bars in screenshots.

- Delete shared screenshots: Automatically delete screenshots after they are shared via the screen toolbar.

- Screenshot format: Select whether you want the screenshots to be saved in JPG or PNG files.

Screensaver

Record activities to your device, record, and capture a video layer of yourself with a camera to share with friends or family.

1. In Quick Settings, tap Screen saver> Start recording.

2. The three-second countdown starts before the recording starts. To start recording immediately, tap Skip countdown.

• To draw on the screen, tap Draw.

• Touch the cursor to display the icon on the screen while using the S Pen (Galaxy S21 Ultra 5G only).

• Touch Selfie Video to turn on footage from the front camera.

3. Touch Stop to end the recording. They are automatically saved in the Screenshots album in Gallery.

Screen Saver Settings

Manage sound recorder and sound quality settings.

○ In Settings, tap Advanced Features> Screenshots and Screensaver.

- Sound: Select the sounds you want to record while using the screen recorder.

-Video quality: select the resolution. Choosing a higher resolution for higher quality requires more memory.

- Video size for selfies: Drag the slider to set the video layer size.

CHAPTER NINE

USING APP

The application list shows all preloaded and downloaded programs. You can download apps from Galaxy and Google Play stores

○ On the start screen, swipe up to open the application list.

Uninstall or Disable Applications

You can remove installed applications from your device. Some preloaded programs (available on your device by default) can only be disabled. Disabled apps are excluded and hidden from the apps list.

○ In apps, tap and hold the app, then tap Remove / Disable.

Searching for Applications

If you are not sure where to find an application or setting, you can use the search function.

1. In the applications, tap Search and enter a word or words. As you type, the corresponding programs and settings appear on the screen.

2. Tap a result to open this app.

TIP You can adjust the search settings by tapping More options> Settings.

Sorting Applications

You can list application shortcuts alphabetically or in order.

◌ In the app, tap More options> Sort for the following sort options:

• Custom: Schedule apps manually.

• Alphabetically: Sort applications alphabetically.

TIP: When you edit programs manually (custom order), you can remove empty icon spaces by tapping More options> Clear pages.

Applications

Creating and using folders

You can create folders to organize shortcuts to applications in the application list.

1. In an app, tap and hold an app shortcut, and drag it to the top of another app shortcut until it's highlighted.

2. Drop the application shortcut to create a folder.

• Folder name: Name the folder.

• Palette: change the color of the folder.

• Add applications: save several applications in a folder. Tap apps to select them, then tap Done.

3. Touch Back to close the folder.

Copy a folder to the Home screen

You can copy a folder to the Home screen.

○ In applications, tap and hold a folder, then tap Add to home.

Delete A Folder

When you delete a folder, application shortcuts return to the application list.

1. In applications, tap and hold the folder you want to delete.

2. Touch Delete folder and confirm when prompted.

Game Booster

Achieve optimized performance while playing games based on usage. Prevent calls and enable features such as Bixby or Dolby

○ While playing a game, slide up from the bottom of the screen to show the navigation bar. The following options are visible on the far right and left:

• Touch screen lock: Lock the screen to prevent accidental touching. This is the default option.

• Game Booster: Configure other options, including performance monitoring and navigation bar blocking, screen touches, and screenshots.

Application Settings

Manage downloaded and preloaded applications. In Settings, tap Apps. Touch customization options:

• Select default apps: select the apps you want to use to make calls, send messages, visit web pages, and more.

• Samsung application settings: View a list of Samsung applications and adjust their settings.

• Your apps: tap the app to view and update information about privacy and user settings. Options vary by application.

Tip to undo changes to apps that have changed, tap More options> Undo app settings.

SAMSUNG APP

Galaxy Essentials

Galaxy Essentials is a collection of specially selected apps available through Samsung Apps. You access a collection of top-notch content and can download it. ○ In Apps, tap More Options> Galaxy Essentials.

AR area

Access all augmented reality (AR) functions in one place. See the AR area for more information.

Bixby

Bixby displays customized content based on your interactions. Bixby learns from your usage patterns and suggests content you might like. See Bixby for more information.

Galaxy Shop

The best way to stay up to date with the following Galaxy devices, buy Samsung products and unlock exclusive offers.

Galaxy Store

Find and download top apps that are exclusive to Galaxy devices. A Samsung account is required to download from the Galaxy Store.

Galaxy Wearable

Connect your device to your Samsung Watch with this app.

Game Launcher

Automatically arrange all your games in one place.

Tip If the Game Launcher does not appear in the list of applications, in the settings, click Advanced Features> Game Launcher and then click.

PENUP

Share photos, comment on other creations, or simply browse the pages and add something to your collection. This community brings together all those who use the S Pen to draw, paint, draw or paint.

Samsung's free

access to TV shows, news, and articles from many sources and interactive games is completely free.

Samsung Global

Goals Learn more about the Global Goals initiative and contribute to donations that support these causes with ads from this app.

Samsung Members

Samsung can preload on your phone or download from the Galaxy Store or Google Play.

Samsung TV Plus

 Enjoy free news, entertainment, and more on Samsung TVs and mobile devices.

SmartThings

SmartThings allows you to control, automate and monitor your home environment via a mobile device that meets your specific needs.

You can connect multiple devices at the same time or to one device at a time.

Check the condition of your devices by looking at the dashboard.

NOTE: Defects or errors of non-Samsung devices are not covered by the Samsung warranty; contact a non-Samsung device manufacturer for support.

Tips See tips and techniques and a user guide for your device.

CALCULATOR

The Calculator application contains basic and scientific mathematical functions and a unit converter.

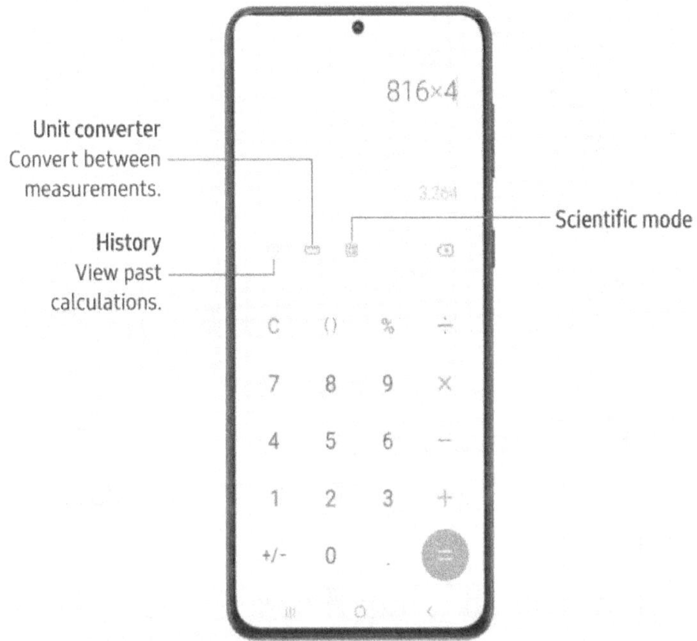

CALENDAR

The Calendar application can connect to different network accounts to combine all calendars in one place.

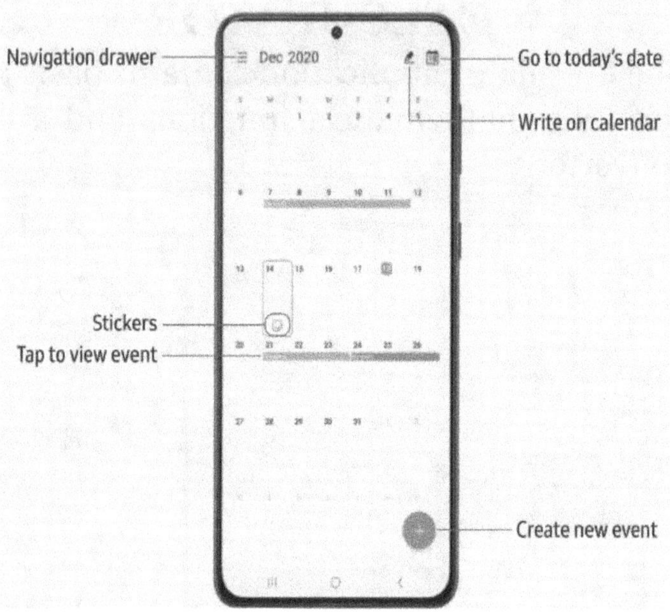

Add a calendar

Add your accounts to the Calendar application.

1. In the calendar, tap the navigation tray.

2. Touch Calendar Settings> Add Account and select an account type.

3. Enter your account information and follow the instructions.

TIP accounts can also support email, contacts, and other features.

Subscribe to Calendars

Subscribe to calendars to suit your interests, you will be able to find various upcoming events and add them to your schedule.

1. In the calendar, tap the navigation tray.

2. Touch Add Your Interests and follow the instructions.

Calendar Alert Style

You can set calendar alerts to different styles.

1. In Calendar, tap the navigation tray> Calendar settings> Alert style. The following options are available:

• Light: receive a notification and hear a short beep.

• Medium: Receive a full-screen warning and hear a short beep.

• Powerful: You will receive a full-screen alert and a ringtone until you release it.

2. Depending on the alert style above, these sound options are available:

• One-tone ringtone: Select a warning sound for a light or medium alert style.

• Ring forward: select a warning sound for a strong alert style.

Creating an Event

Create an event with your calendar.

1. In the calendar, tap Add event to add an event.

2. Enter the event details and tap Save.

Delete events

Delete events from the calendar.

1. In Calendar, tap an event, then tap again to edit it.

2. Touch Delete and confirm when prompted.

Clock

The Clock application provides time tracking and alarm settings.

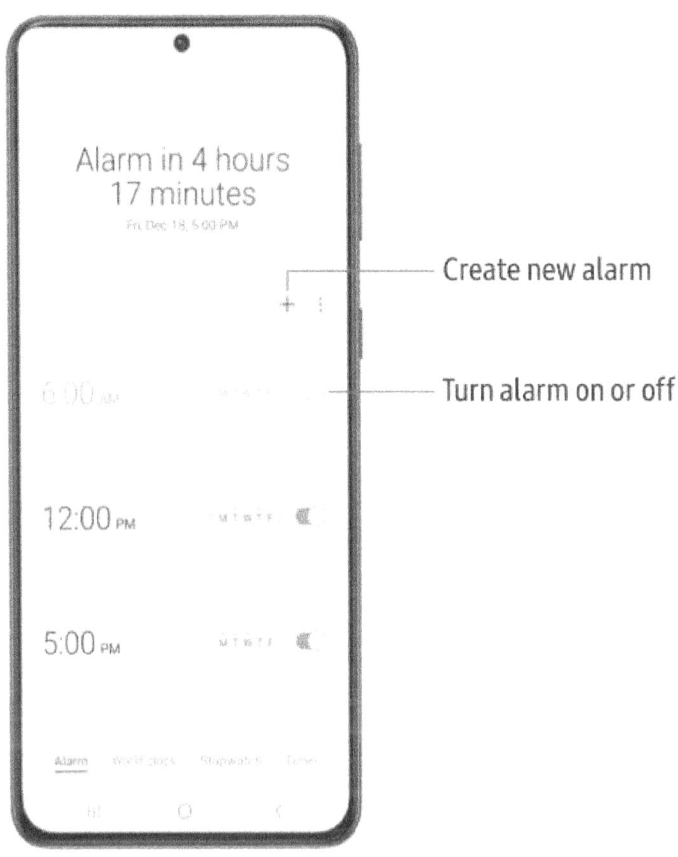

Alarm

Use the Alarm tab to set one-time or recurring alarms and select notification options.

1. On the watch, click add an alarm.

2. Touch the following items to configure the alarm:

• Time: set the alarm time.

• Day: select days for this alarm.

• Alarm name: enter the alarm name.

• Alarm sound: select the sound to sound the alarm and drag the slider to adjust the alarm volume.

• Vibrate: Select whether the alarm uses vibration.

• Delay: allow delay. Set the interval and alarm repeat values during the delay.

3. Touch Save to save the alarm.

Deleting an alarm

1. On the watch, press and drag the alarm.

2. Touch Delete.

Alert settings

You can set the device to vibrate for alarms and timers, regardless of whether the sound mode is set to Silent or Vibrate.

1. On the watch, tap More options> Settings.

2. Touch Vibrate for alarms and countdowns to enable the feature.

CHAPTER TEN

CONTACT APP

Store and manage contacts. You can sync with the personal accounts added to your device. Accounts can also support email, calendars, and other features.

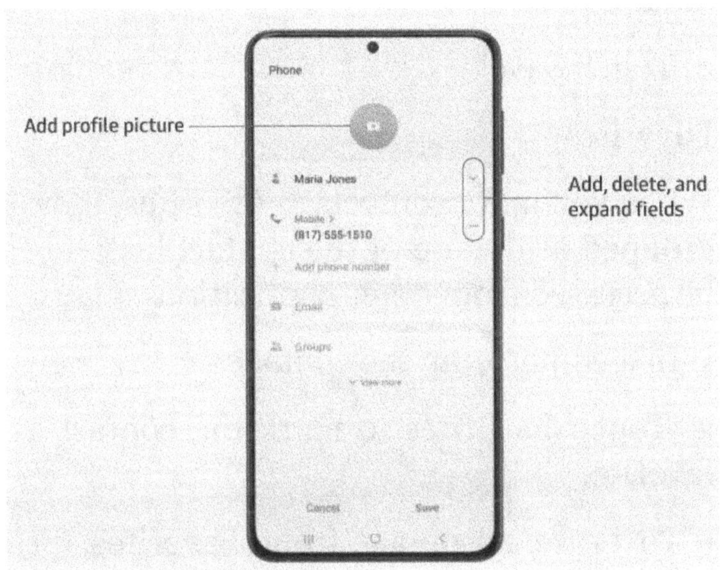

Create a contact

1. In Contacts, tap Create contact.

2. Enter your contact information and tap Save.

Editing a contact

While editing a contract, you can tap a field to change or delete information, or add more fields to your contact information list.

1. In a contact, click the contact.

2. Touch Edit.

3. Touch any box to add, change, or delete data.

4. Touch Save.

Favorites

When you mark contacts as favorites, they are grouped at the top of the contact list and can be accessed from other applications.

1. In a contact, tap the contact.

2. Touch Favorites to mark the contact as a favorite.

• To erase a contact from Favorites, press Favorites.

Share A Contact

Share with others using a variety of sharing methods and services.

1. In a contact, tap the contact.

2. Touch Sharing.

3. Touch File or Text.

4. Select a sharing method and follow the instructions.

TIP While viewing a contact, tap More options> QR code to quickly share information with friends or family.

The QR code is automatically updated when you change the contact information fields.

Show content-sharing contacts
Share content directly with contacts from any app. When enabled, your frequent contacts appear in the Sharing window.

◦ In Settings, tap Advanced features> Show content sharing contacts, then tap to enable the feature.

Create a group
Create your contact groups.

1. In the phonebook, tap Open tray> Groups.

2. Click Create group and then the fields for entering group information:

• Group name: put a name for the group.

• Group ringtone: adjust the sounds for the group.

• Add member: select the contacts you want to add to the new group, then tap Done.

3. Touch Save.

Add or remove contacts in a group

○ In the Contacts menu, open Tray> Groups and tap a group.

• To remove a contact, touch and hold the contact to select it, then tap Remove.

• To add a contact, tap Edit> Add member, then tap the contacts you want to add. When you're done, tap Done> Save.

Send a message to a group

Send a text message to the members of the group.

1. In Contacts, tap Open tray> Groups, then tap a group.

2. Touch More Options> Send Message.

Email group members.

1. In Contacts, tap Open tray> Groups, then tap a group.

2. Touch More Options> Send Email.

3. Click the contacts to select them, or press all check box at the top of the screen to select all, and then click Done.

• Only group members who have an email address in their records are displayed.

4. Select an email account and follow the instructions.

Delete group

Delete the group you created.

1. In Contacts, tap Open tray> Groups, then tap a group.

2. Touch More Options> Delete.

• To delete a group only, tap Group.

• To delete a group and group contacts, tap Group and members.

Managing Contacts

You can import or export contacts and combine multiple contacts into one contact entry.

Merge Contacts

Merge contact information from multiple sources into one contact by linking the entries to one contact.

1. In the phonebook, tap Open Tray> Manage Contacts.

2. Touch Merge Contacts. Contacts with double phone numbers, email addresses, and names will be listed together.

3. Tap contacts to select them, then tap Connect.

Delete Duplicate Contacts

Quickly remove duplicate contacts.

1. In the phonebook, tap Open Tray> Manage Contacts.

2. Touch Delete Duplicate Contacts. Duplicate contacts are listed.

3. Click contacts to choose them, and then click erase.

Import Contacts

Import contacts to your device as a vCard (VCF) file.

1. In the phonebook, tap Open Tray> Manage Contacts.

2. Touch Import or Export Contacts.

3. Touch Import and follow the instructions.

Export Contacts

Exports contacts from the device as a vCard (VCF) file.

1. In the phonebook, tap Open Tray> Manage Contacts.

2. Touch Import or Export Contacts.

3. Touch Export and follow the instructions.

Synchronizing Contacts

Update all contacts in all accounts regularly.

1. In the phonebook, tap Open Tray> Manage Contacts.

2. Touch Sync Contacts.

Set The Default Storage Location

Automatically save new contacts to your device, SIM card, or account.

1. In the phonebook, tap Open Tray> Manage Contacts.

2. Touch Set Default Storage Location.

3. Touch or add an account to set the default.

Delete contacts

Delete one or more contacts.

1. In the phonebook, touch and hold a contact to select it.

• You can also touch other contacts to select them to delete.

2. Touch Delete and confirm when prompted.

CHAPTER ELEVEN

INTERNET APP

Samsung Internet is a very easy, fast, and sure web browser for your device. Experience more secure web browsing features with hidden mode, biometric sign-in, and content blocking.

Browser Tabs

Use tabs to browse several web pages at once.

○ On the Internet, click tabs> New tab.

• To close a tab, press Tabs-Close Tab.

Bookmark

Select your favorite sites for quick access.

○ On the Internet, tap Mark to save the open web page.

Open A Bookmark

 Quickly launch a webpage from the bookmarks page.

1. On the Internet, tap Bookmarks.

2. Touch the label entry.

Saving A Website

There are several options for saving a website in the Samsung web application.

○ On the Internet, click Tools> Add page for the following options:

• Bookmarks: Add the web page to the bookmarks list.

• Quick access: view a list of frequently accessed or saved web pages.

• Home screen: create a shortcut to a web page on the home screen.

• Saved pages: Save the content of the web page to your device so that you can access it offline.

View History

To view a list of recently visited web pages: ○
On the Internet, tap Tools> History.

Tip-To erases your browsing history, press
more options> clear history.

Sharing Pages

You can share web pages with your contacts.

○ On the Internet, tap Tools> Share, and
follow the instructions.

Secret Mode

The pages you view in secret mode are not
listed in your browser history or search history
and do not leave traces (such as cookies) on
your device.

Secret cards are darker in color than regular
card windows.

All downloaded files remain on the device
when you close the secret card.

1. On the Internet, tap the tabs> Turn on secret
mode.

2. Touch Start to start browsing in secret
mode.

Secret mode settings

To use secret mode, you need a password or a biometric lock.

1. Tap tabs on the Internet.

2. Touch More Options> Secret Mode Settings for the following options:

• Use Password: Create a password to enable hidden mode.

• Face: Use face recognition to keep the secret mode private.

• Fingerprint: Use a fingerprint scanner to maintain privacy in secret mode.

• Clear secret mode: delete the secret mode data and restore the default settings.

Turn Off Secret Mode

Disable hidden mode and return to normal browsing.

○ On the Internet, click the tabs> Turn off hidden mode.

Internet Settings

Change the settings related to using the Internet application.

○ On the Internet, tap Tools> Settings

CHAPTER TWELVE

MESSAGE APP AND MY FILES

Keep in touch with your Messages app to share photos, send emojis, or simply say hello.

○ In the message, tap Compose a new message.

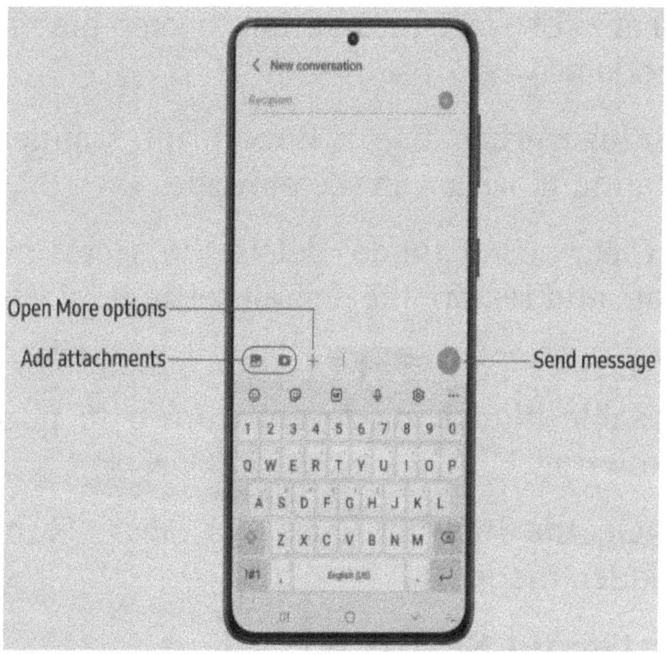

Searching for messages

To find a message quickly, use the search function.

1. In the message, tap Search.

2. Enter keywords in the search box, then tap
Keyboard search.

Delete Conversations

You can delete conversion history
conversations.

1. In the message, tap More options> Delete.

2. Touch each conversation you want to delete.

3. Touch Delete All and confirm when
prompted.

Sending Sos Messages

In an emergency, send a message with your
location to a specific contact.

1. In Settings, tap Advanced Features> Send
SOS Messages, then tap to enable this feature.

• To select how many times you press the side
key to send an SOS message, tap 3 or 4 times.

• To select the contact you want to call
automatically after sending the SOS message,
tap Call someone automatically.

• To include an image from the front and rear
cameras, tap Attach images.

• To include a five-second sound clip in the
SOS message, tap Attach sound.

• To add recipients by creating new contacts or choosing Contacts, tap Send messages.

2. Press the side key quickly or three times to send an SOS message.

Message Settings

Configure settings for text and multimedia messages.

○ In the message, tap More options> Settings.

Emergency Alerts

Emergency alerts alert you to imminent threats and other situations. It is not necessary to receive an emergency message.

1. In Settings, tap Notifications> Advanced Settings.

2. Touch Wireless Emergency Alerts to customize emergency alerts.

MY FILES

You can also access and manage files stored in cloud accounts.

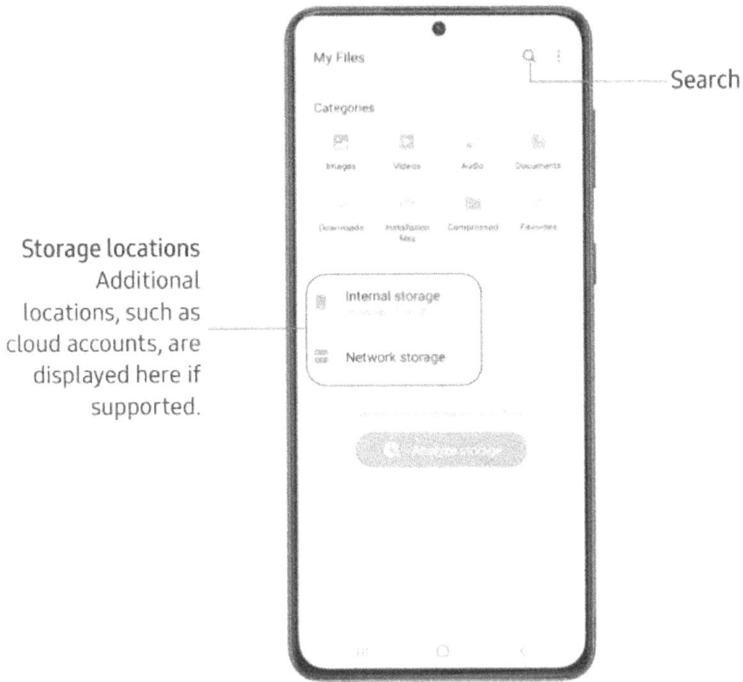

Filegroups

Files stored on your device are grouped into the following groups:

• Recent files: View recently available files.

• Categories: browse files by file type.

• Storage: View files stored on your device and cloud accounts.

- Cloud accounts vary depending on the services you log in to.

• Analyze memory: see what takes up space in your memory.

My File Options

Use My files to search, edit, clear file history, and more.

○ The following options are available in the My files menu:

• Search: find a file.

• More options:

- Cloud service: If available, connect to the mobile operator's cloud service.

- Clear recent files list: erase the list of currently accessed files. This option is only ready after opening a file via My Files.

- Analyze memory: see what takes up space in your memory.

- Trash: Select to restore or permanently delete files that you have deleted.

- Settings: display application settings.

- Contact us: contact Samsung members (if supported by your operator).

CHAPTER THIRTEEN

PHONE CALL APP AND SAMSUNG HEALTH

The Phone application is more than just a phone call. Explore advanced calling features. Contact your network operator for more information. The actual appearance of the phone application screen varies by operator.

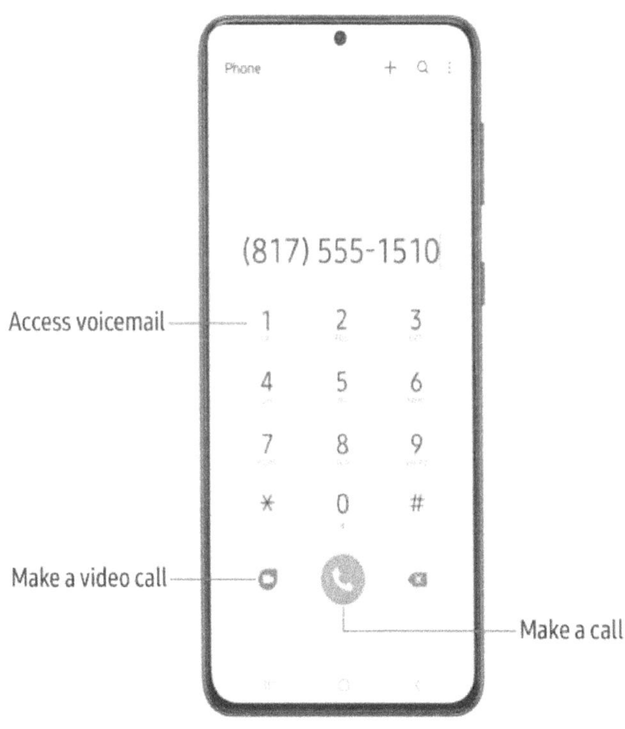

Calls

The phone application allows you to make and receive calls from the Home screen, the Recent tab, Contacts, and more.

Making A Call

You can make and receive calls from the home screen with your phone.

○ Enter the number on the phone keypad and click Call.

• Touch the keyboard if the keyboard is not displayed.

Making Calls from Recent Calls

All incoming, outgoing and missed calls are entered.

1. In your phone, tap Recent to view a list of recent calls.

2. Tap a contact, then tap Call.

Calling from the phonebook

Call a contact from contacts.

○ In the Contacts menu, swipe right after the contact to call the contact.

Answer A Call

When you receive a call, the phone rings, and the caller's phone number or name is displayed.

If you are using the application, an incoming call pop-up screen is displayed.

○ On the incoming call screen, swipe Answer to the right to answer the call.

Tip On the incoming call pop-up screen, press answer the call.

Rejecting A Call

You can reject an incoming call. If you are using the application, an incoming call pop-up screen is displayed.

○ On the incoming call screen, drag Reject left to reject the call and send it to voicemail.

Reject with Message

You can reject an incoming call with an SMS message.

○ On the incoming call screen, drag Send message up and select a message.

Tip On the incoming call pop-up screen, click send a message and choose a message.

Ending a call

○ When you are ready to make a call, tap End.

Actions During A Call

During a call, you can adjust the call volume, switch to headset or speakerphone, and even multitask.

-Click the volume keys to enlarge or decrease the volume.

Switch to A Headset or Speaker

Listen to a call using a Bluetooth® speaker or headset (not supplied).

○ Touch Loudspeaker to hear the caller through the loudspeaker or tap Bluetooth to hear it through the Bluetooth headset.

Multitasking

If you leave the call screen and use another application, your active call is displayed in the status bar.

To return to the call screen:

○ Drag the status bar downwards to display the notification panel, and tap the call.

To end a call during multitasking:

○ Drag the status bar down to display a notification panel, then tap End call.

Call background

Select an image or video to display while making or receiving a call.

○ On your phone, tap More options> Settings> Call background for the following options:

• Appearance: Select how the caller information is displayed when the person has a profile picture.

• Wallpaper: select a photo to display during a call.

Pop-Up Settings

When calls are received while using other applications, they may appear as pop-ups.

○ On your phone, while tapping applications, tap More options> Settings> Call screen. The following options are available:

• Full-screen view: View the incoming call in the Phone application in full screen.

• Mini pop-up: View an incoming call as a smaller pop-up.

• Hold calls in pop-ups: Enable this option to put calls in pop-ups after answering.

Call Handling

Your calls are recorded in the call log. You can set up speed dialing, block numbers, and use voicemail.

Call list

The phone numbers you have called, received, or missed are saved in the call log.

○ Touch Recent on your phone. A list of recent calls is displayed. If the caller is on your contact list, the caller's name is displayed.

Save a contact from a recent call

Use recent call information to create a contact or update your contact list.

1. On your phone, tap Recent.

2. Tap the call that contains the information you want to save to your contact list, then tap Add to contacts.

3. Touch Create New Contact or Update Existing Contact.

Delete the call log

To delete a call log entry:

1. On your phone, tap Recent.

2. Click and drag the call you want to erase from the call log.

3. Touch Delete.

Blocking A Number

If you add a caller to the blocked list, future calls from that number will be sent directly to your voicemail and no messages will be received.

1. On your phone, tap Recent.

2. Touch the caller you want to add to the blocked list.

3. Tap Details> Block and confirm when prompted.

Tip You can also change the blocked list in the settings. On your phone, tap More options> Settings> Block numbers.

Speed Dialling

You can assign a number to speed dialing shortcuts.

1. In your phone, tap Keyboard> More options> Speed dial numbers. The speed dial screen shows the reserved speed dial numbers.

2. Touch an unassigned number.

• Touch Menu to select another speed dial number from the next in sequence.

• Number 1 is reserved for voicemail.

3. Enter a name or number or tap Add among contacts to assign a contact to the number.

• The selected contact appears in the speed dial field.

Speed dialling

You can make a speed dialling call. ◌ Touch and hold a speed dial number on your phone.

• If the speed dial number is more than one number, enter the first number and hold the last number.

Removing a speed dial number

You can remove the assigned speed dial number.

1. In your phone, tap More options> Speed dial numbers.

2. Touch Delete next to the contact you want to remove from the speed dial.

Emergency calls

You can call an emergency number in your region, regardless of the phone service status.

If the phone is not activated, you can only make emergency calls.

1. Enter the emergency number (911 in North America) for your phone and tap Call.

2. End the call. During this type of call, you have access to most functions during a call.

TIP You can call an emergency number even when the phone is locked, allowing anyone to use your phone and call for help. When you access the lock screen, only the emergency call function is available to the caller. The rest of the phone is still secured.

Phone Settings

These settings allow you to change the settings related to the Phone application.

⊙ On your phone, tap More options> Settings.

Optional call services

Your network operator and service package may support the following call services.

Multi-page dialing

Make another call during a call. Options vary by operator.

1. In an active call, tap Add call to make a new call.

2. Call the new number and tap Call. When a call is answered:

• Click swap to switch between the two calls.

• Click a number to switch between the two calls.

• Touch Connect to hear both callers at the same time (multiple conferences).

Video Calls

To make video calls:

○ Touch the phone, enter the number, and then tap Duo call or Video call or Video call.

NOTE Video calls are not supported on all devices. The receiver can answer a video call or answer a call as a normal voice call.

Real-Time Text (RTT)

Enter back and forth with the other person during the call.

You can use RTT at any time to call someone whose phone also supports RTT or is connected to a Teletext recorder (TTY).

The RTT icon shows all incoming calls.

1. On your phone, tap More options> Settings.

2. Touch real-time text for the following options:

• RTT call button: Select the visibility option of the RTT call button.

• Always visible: Display the RTT call button on the keypad and during a call.

• TTY mode: select the desired TTY mode for the keyboard you are using.

SAMSUNG HEALTH

Use Samsung Health to plan, monitor various aspects of daily life that contribute to well-being, such as physical activity, diet, and sleep. **Note** The information collected on this device, Samsung Health, or related software is not intended to be used in diagnosing disease or other conditions or in treating, alleviating, treating, or preventing disease.

The accuracy of the information and data provided by this device and related software may be affected by factors such as environmental conditions, certain activity performed during use - transfer of the device, device settings, user configuration - information provided by the device. user, and other end users. user interactions.

Before You Start Exercising

Although the Samsung Health app is a great companion to your exercise routine, it is always advisable to consult your doctor before any exercise regimen.

If a moderate physical activity, such as brisk walking, is safe for most people, healthcare professionals suggest that you talk to your doctor before you start exercising, especially if you have any of the following conditions:

• heart disease; Asthma or lung disease; diabetes or liver or kidney disease; in arthritis.

Talk to your doctor before starting exercise if you have symptoms that indicate heart, lung, or other serious illness, such as:

• dizziness or loss of consciousness;

• difficulty breathing with light exertion or at rest or while lying down or sleeping;

• swelling of the ankle, especially at night;

• Heart murmur or rapid or pronounced heartbeat;

• Muscle aches while walking up or up and goes away when you rest.

It is recommended that you consult your doctor before exercising.

If you are unsure of your health, have more health problems, or are pregnant,

CHAPTER FOURTEEN

SAMSUNG NOTE AND SAMSUNG PAY

You can easily share notes with social networking services.

Create notes

Add text, pictures, voice recordings, and more.

1. In Samsung Notes, tap Add.

2. Use text options to create content.

Voice Recordings

Create recorded voice recordings that are perfect for lectures or meetings.

Make a note while recording sound. Playback is synchronized to scroll to the corresponding text.

1. In Samsung Notes, tap Add.

2. Touch Insert> Voice Recordings.

3. Use text options to create content while recording audio.

Edit Notes

Edit the notes you have created.

1. In Samsung Notes, tap a note to view it.

2. Touch Edit and make changes.

3. Touch More options for the following:

• Share: select a file type and share a note.

• Save as file: select to save the note as a Samsung Note, PDF, Microsoft Word, Microsoft PowerPoint, image, or text file.

• Sort pages: add, cut, and erase pages.

• Page template: use a template for some or all pages.

• Background color: Use the color page.

• Add to Favorites / Remove from Favorites: Notes are saved in the Favorites folder in the Notes menu.

• Add bookmarks / Edit bookmarks: use bookmarks to easily find notes.

• Finger drawing/finger drawing: enable finger drawing. If disabled, you can only use the S Pen (Galaxy S21 Ultra 5G only) to draw.

4. If done, press back.

Note options

You can edit, sort, or manage notes. The following options are available in Samsung Notes:

• Import PDF files: Open PDF in Samsung Notes.

• Search: search for a keyword.

• More options:

- Edit: select the notes you want to share, delete, save as a file, lock, or move.

- Sort: change the way you edit notes.

Note Menu

You can view the Notes menu by category.

○ In Samsung Notes, tap the navigation tray for the following options:

• Settings: view Samsung Notes settings.

• All notes: view all notes.

• Frequently used: quick access to frequently used notes.

• Shared notebooks: View shared notebooks with contacts through your Samsung account.

• Trash: erased notes for up to 15 days.

• Folders: view notes by groups.

SAMSUNG PAY

Samsung Pay allows you to pay through your device. It's accepted almost anywhere you can swipe your finger or touch a credit card.

Note for added security, your credit and debit card information is not stored in the cloud service. If you use the Samsung Pay application on more than one device, you must log in to the application and confirm all payment cards on each device.

Using Samsung Pay

Use Samsung Pay by opening the app and holding the device above the card reader in the store.

1. In the Samsung Pay app, select the card you want to play with and approve the payment by scanning your finger or entering your Samsung Pay PIN.

2. Hold the phone over the memory card reader.

• When the payment is completed, the invoice will be sent to your registered email address.

Note Make sure NFC is enabled on your device. See NFC and Payment for more information.

Quick Access

With quick access, open Samsung Pay from the lock screen, home screen, or off.

1. In Samsung Pay, click Menu> Settings> Quick access.

2. Touch to enable each screen option.

To use Quick Access:

1. Slide up from the bottom of the screen to any screen.

• Your card quick access is showed.

2. Pull the card down to close Quick Access.

Use Gift Cards with Samsung Pay

Buy, send, and redeem gift cards from a growing selection of your favorite merchants.

Protect Your Data

Samsung Pay is designed with the latest security technology and works on the latest Samsung Galaxy devices.

Payments are approved with a fingerprint or PIN, and each transaction uses a unique token each time, so the device only allows payments with your consent.

If the device is ever lost, you can use the Find My Cell Phone Remote feature to delete data for even greater protection.

CHAPTER FIFTEEN

GOOGLE AND MICROSOFT APPS

Chrome

Browse the web with Chrome ™ and transfer open tabs, bookmarks, and address bar data from your computer to your mobile device. Visit support.google.com/chrome for more information.

Drive

Open, view, rename, and share files stored in your Google Drive cloud account ™. Visit support.google.com/drive for more information.

Duo

Make video calls. Visit support.google.com/duo for more information.

Gmail

Send and receive an email with Google's online email service. To learn more, visit support.google.com/mail.

Google

Search for online content with tools that teach you what interests you. Turn on your custom source to receive custom content.

Google Pay

 Pay with your Android phone in participating stores and mobile applications with Google Pay

Maps

Get directions and other location information. Enable location to use Google Maps.

Photos

Save and automatically back up your photos and videos to your Google Account with Google Photos

Play Movies and Tv

Watch movies and TV shows bought on Google Play. You can also look at videos stored on your device.

Play Store

Find recent apps, movies and TV shows, games, books, magazines, and more in the Google Play Store.

MICROSOFT APPS

Outlook

Access email, contacts, and more in Outlook

LinkedIn

Connect and connect with other professionals around the world.

Office

Enjoy Word, Excel, and PowerPoint on your mobile device with the Microsoft Office mobile app.

OneDrive

Save and share photos, videos, documents, and more in your free OneDrive® online account - which you can access from your PC, tablet, or phone.

CHAPTER SIXTEEN

SETTINGS

Access settings

- On the Home screen, slide your finger down and tap Settings.

- In the applications, tap Settings. Searching for settings If you are not sure where to find a particular setting, you can search for it.

1. In the settings, tap Search and enter keywords.

2. Touch an entry to switch to this setting.

Connections

Manage connections between your device and various networks and other devices.

Wi-Fi

You can connect your device to a Wi-Fi network to access the Internet without using mobile data.

1. In Settings, tap Connections> Wi-Fi, then tap to turn on Wi-Fi and search for available networks.

2. Touch the network and enter a password, if required.

Connecting to a hidden Wi-Fi network

If the desired Wi-Fi network is not listed after scanning, you can still connect to manual data entry.

Before you begin, ask your Wi-Fi administrator for your username and password.

1. In Settings, tap Connections> Wi-Fi, then tap to turn on Wi-Fi.

2. Click add network at the bottom of the list.

3. Enter the Wi-Fi network information:

• Network name: enter the correct network name.

• Security: Select a security option from the list and enter a password if required.

4. Touch Save.

Tip Touch the QR scanner button to connect to a Wi-Fi network with the QR code scanner camera.

Advanced Wi-Fi settings

In your device, you can configure connections to different types of Wi-Fi networks and access points, manage saved networks, and search for network addresses. Options may vary by operator.

1. In Settings, tap Connections> Wi-Fi, then tap to turn on Wi-Fi.

2. Touch More Options> Advanced.

• Switch to mobile data: If enabled, the device will switch to mobile data when the Wi-Fi connection is unstable.

  When the Wi-Fi signal is strong, it returns to Wi-Fi.

• Turn on Wi-Fi automatically: Turn on Wi-Fi infrequently used places.

• Suspicious network detection: Receive a notification when suspicious activity is detected on the current Wi-Fi network.

• Show network quality information: See network information (such as speed and stability) in the list of available Wi-Fi networks.

• Wi-Fi power saving mode: Enable Wi-Fi traffic analysis to reduce battery consumption.

• Network notifications / Wi-Fi notifications: Receive notifications when you detect open networks within range.

• Show Wi-Fi pop-up: Notify me that Wi-Fi is available when opening apps.

• Network management: view saved Wi-Fi networks and set whether to automatically reconnect to individual networks or forget them.

• Wi-Fi control history: View programs that have recently turned Wi-Fi on or off.

• Hotspot 2.0: Automatically connect to Wi-Fi networks that support Hotspot 2.0.

• Install network certificates: Install certificates for authentication.

Wi-Fi Direct

Wi-Fi Direct uses Wi-Fi to exchange data between devices.

1. In Settings, tap Connections> Wi-Fi, then tap to turn on Wi-Fi.

2. Touch More Options> Wi-Fi Direct.

3. Touch the device and follow the connection instructions.

Disconnect the device from Wi-Fi Direct.

In Settings, tap Connections> Wi-Fi> More options> Wi-Fi Direct. Touch the device to disconnect it.

Bluetooth

You can pair your device with other Bluetooth-enabled devices, such as a Bluetooth headset or a Bluetooth-enabled infotainment system.

Once the pairing is created, the devices are remembered and can exchange data without re-entering the access code.

1. In Settings, tap Connections> Bluetooth, then tap to turn on Bluetooth.

2. Touch the device and follow the connection instructions.

TIP While sharing a file, press Bluetooth to use this feature.

Rename A Paired Device

You can rename a paired device to help identify it.

1. In Settings, tap Connections> Bluetooth, then tap to turn on Bluetooth.

2. Touch Settings next to the device name, then tap Rename.

3. Enter a new name and tap Rename.

Disconnect a Bluetooth device

When you pair it with a Bluetooth device, both devices no longer recognize it, so you need to pair it again.

1. In Settings, click Connections> Bluetooth, then tap to turn on Bluetooth.

2. Click Settings next to the device, and then click Schedule.

Advanced Options

Additional Bluetooth functions are available in the Advanced menu. Options may vary by operator.

1. In Settings, press Connections> Bluetooth.

2. Touch More Options> Advanced or Advanced for the following options:

-Sync with Samsung Cloud: Sync files downloaded via Bluetooth with your Samsung account.

-Phone name: change the name of the Bluetooth device.

-Files received: View a list of files received via Bluetooth.

- Music sharing: Allow friends to play music through a Bluetooth speaker or headset.

-Ring sync: Use the ringtone set on your device when receiving calls through a connected Bluetooth device.

- Bluetooth control history: View applications that have recently used Bluetooth.

Dual Audio

You can play audio from your device on two connected Bluetooth audio devices.

1. Connect Bluetooth audio devices to the device.

2. On the notification panel, tap Media.

3. In the Audio Output section, tap next to each audio device to play audio (up to two devices).

NFC and Nearby Payment

 communication (NFC) allows you to communicate with another device without connecting to the network.

This technology is used by Android Beam and some payment applications.

The device you are transferring to must support NFC and be no more than 4 cm away from your device.

○ In Settings, tap Connections> NFC and contactless payments, then tap to turn on this feature.

Tap and pay

With the NFC payment application, you can pay by tapping your device with a compatible credit card reader.

1. In Settings, tap Connections> NFC and contactless payments, then tap to turn on NFC.

2. Touch Contactless Payment to display the default payment application.

• To use another payment app, tap an available app to select it.

• To use an open app for payment, tap Payment with the app currently open.

• To set another payment service as the default, tap Other and then the desired service.

TYPE NFC technology is used with Samsung Pay. Turn on this feature to see how easy and secure it is to use your payment device.

Flight Mode

Flight mode turns off all network connections, including calling, messaging, mobile data, Wi-Fi, and Bluetooth. When airplane mode is enabled, you can turn on Wi-Fi and Bluetooth in Settings or the Quick Settings panel.

◌ In Settings, tap Connections> Airplane mode, then tap to enable this feature.

Mobile Networks

Use mobile networks to configure your device to connect to mobile networks and use mobile data. Options may vary by operator.

◌ In Settings, tap Connections> Mobile networks.

• Mobile data: enable the use of mobile data.

• International data roaming: change the voice, text, and data roaming settings for international roaming.

• Allow 2G service: Allow the use of 2G service in areas with limited mobile coverage.

• Data roaming: Select whether you want to allow the device to connect to mobile data when you travel outside your network area.

• Roaming / Roaming status: enable or disable data when roaming on other mobile networks.

• Signal strength: View the signal strength of the mobile signal.

• Enhanced dialling: Enable enhanced communication using LTE data.

• **Network mode:** You can choose which network modes your phone can use.

• System selection: change the CDMA roaming mode if appropriate for your operator.

• Access point names: Select or add APNs with network settings that your device must connect to the service provider.

• Network operators: select available and desired networks.

• Mobile network diagnostics: Collect diagnostic and usage data for troubleshooting.

• Network Extender: Find stations that can extend your network connection.

TIP Use these features to manage connection settings that may affect your monthly bill.

Data Usage

Check the current data usage for mobile and Wi-Fi. You can also customize alerts and restrictions.

In Settings, tap Connections> Data usage.

Turn On Data Saving

Use data saving to reduce data usage by preventing selected applications from sending or receiving data in the background.

1. In Settings, tap Connections> Data usage> Data storage.

2. Touch to turn on Data Storage.

• To allow some apps to use data indefinitely, tap Allow data usage while saving data is turned on, then tap next to each app to set restrictions.

Monitoring Mobile Data

You can customize access to mobile data by setting restrictions and restrictions. Options may vary by operator.

In Settings, tap Connections> Data usage. The following options are available:

• Mobile data: use the mobile data from your plan.

• International data roaming: enable mobile data services during international roaming.

• Mobile data applications: Set the applications to always use mobile data, even if your device is connected to a Wi-Fi network.

• Notify me of data consumption: enable alerts when mobile data consumption reaches the selected amount.

• Mobile data usage: look at data usage over some time.

• Billing cycle and data alert: change the monthly date to match the billing date of your mobile operator.

TIP Use these features to monitor data usage estimates.

Wi-Fi Data

control You can restrict access to Wi-Fi data by customizing usage and network restrictions.

1. In Settings, tap Connections> Data usage.

2. Touch Wi-Fi Data Usage to display data usage over Wi-Fi connections for a specific period. You can see the total spend and the cost per application.

Data Consumption While Roaming

You can monitor data consumption while roaming outside your operator's network.

1. In Settings, tap Connections> Data usage.

2. Touch Use data while roaming to view data usage if and when the device is roaming.

Mobile Access Point

A mobile access point uses your data packet to create a Wi-Fi network that can be used by multiple devices.

1. In Settings, tap Connections> Mobile access point and tethering> Mobile access point.

2. Touch to turn on the mobile access point.

3. Activate Wi-Fi on the devices you want to connect and select the Mobile access point on your device.

  Enter the password of the mobile access point you want to connect to.

• Connected devices are listed in the Connected devices section.

TIP Touch the QR code to connect another device to the mobile contact point by scanning the QR code instead of entering the password.

Changing the mobile access point password

You can customize the mobile access point password to make it easier to remember.

1. In Sting, tap Connections> Mobile access point and mooring> Mobile access point.

2. Touch a password, enter a new password, and tap Save.

Configuring mobile access point settings

You can adjust the security settings and connections of the mobile access point.

1. In Sting, tap Connections> Mobile access point and mooring> Mobile access point.

2. Touch Configuration for the following settings:

• Network name: view and change the name of your mobile access point.

• Security: select the security level for the mobile access point.

• Password: If you select a security level that uses a password, you can view or change it.

• Bandwidth: select one of the available bandwidth options.

• Advanced: configure additional mobile access point settings.

Automatic Access Point

Automatically shares your access point with other devices logged into your Samsung account.

1. In Settings, tap Connections> Mobile access point and tethering> Mobile access point.

2. Touch the autofocus point and tap to enable the feature.

Connectivity

You can use a connection to share your device's Internet connection with another device. Options may vary by operator.

1. In Settings, tap Connections> Mobile access point and mooring.

2. Touch:

• Touch a Bluetooth modem connection to share the device's Internet connection over the Internet.

• Connect the computer to the device with a USB cable, then touch the USB modem connection.

• Connect your computer to the device with an Ethernet interface and tap Ethernet connection.

Scan A Nearby Device

Easily connect to other available devices by turning on nearby device scanning.

 This function notifies you when attachments are available.

1. In Settings, tap Connections> Advanced connection settings> Scan nearby devices.

2. Touch to turn on the function.

Connect To A Printer

Connect your device to a printer on the same Wi-Fi network for easier printing of documents and images from the device.

1. In Settings, touch Connections> Advanced Connection Settings> Print.

2. Touch Default Print Service, and then touch More Options> Add Printer.

• If your printer needs a plug-in, touch Download Plug-in and follow the instructions to add a print service.

Note Not all applications support printing.

Virtual Private Networks

Virtual private networks (VPNs) allow you to connect to a private secure network from your device. You will need a VPN administrator to connect.

1. In Settings, tap Connections> Advanced Connection Settings> VPN.

2. Touch More Options> Add VPN Profile.

3. Enter the VPN information provided by your network administrator and tap Save.

VPN Management

1. In Settings, tap Connections> Advanced Connection Settings> VPN.

2. Touch Settings next to VPN.

3. Edit the VPN and click Save or press Delete.

Connecting to a VPN

Once you have set up a VPN, connecting to and disconnecting from a VPN is very simple.

1. In Settings, press Connections> Advanced Connection Settings> VPN.

2. Click VPN, enter your login information, and click Connect.

- To end the connection, press VPN, then tap Disconnect.

Private DNS

You can connect to a personal DNS host.

1. In Settings, touch Connections> Advanced Connection Settings> Private DNS.

2. Touch one of the available options to configure a private DNS connection.

3. Touch Save.

Ethernet

If a wireless network connection is not available, you can use an Ethernet cable to connect your device to a local area network.

1. Connect the Ethernet cable to your device.

2. In Settings, tap Connections> Advanced Connection Settings> Ethernet and follow the instructions.

TIP You need an adapter (not supplied) to connect the Ethernet cable to the device.

Network Unlock

View the network lock status of your device and make sure it meets the unlock requirements for use on another mobile network. Options may vary by operator.

○ In Settings, tap Connections> Advanced connection settings> Network unlock for the following options:

• Network lock status: View your device's current network lock status.

• Permanent unlock: require permanent network unlock before you can use your device with other service providers.

• Temporary unlock: request a temporary network unlock before you can use your device with other service providers.

CHAPTER SEVENTEEN

SOUND-VIBRATION AND NOTIFICATION

Sound Mode

○ In the settings, tap Sounds & vibrations, then select a mode:

• Sound: Use the sounds, vibrations, and volume you selected in the sound settings for notifications and alerts.

- Vibrate on ringtone: Set the device to vibrate with a ringtone when you receive a call.

• Vibration: Use vibration only for notifications and warnings.

• Mute: Set the device not to emit sounds.

- Pause: set a time limit for switching off the device.

Tip Use the sound mode setting instead of the volume keys to change the sound mode without losing the custom sound level.

Mute Gestures

Mute the sound quickly by covering the display or turning the device.

◌ In Settings, tap Advanced Features> Gestures & Gestures> Turn Off Gestures, then tap to enable.

Vibration

You can control how and when the device vibrates.

1. In the settings, tap Sounds & vibrations.

2. Touch customization options:

• Call vibration pattern: Select one of the pre-set call vibration patterns.

• Notification vibration pattern: select one of the pre-set vibration patterns for notifications.

Volume

Adjust the volume of ringtones, notifications, media, and system sounds.

○ In Settings, tap Sounds & vibrations> Volume and drag the sliders for each sound type.

Tip You can also use the volume keys to change the volume. When you click, the volume level and the current sound type are showed in the pop-up menu.

To touch the menu, expand it, and then change the volume of other types of sound by dragging the sliders.

Using the media volume keys

Set the default volume key action to control the volume of the media sound instead of any type of sound.

1. In Settings, tap Sounds & vibrations> Volume.

2. Touch Use Media Volume key to enable this feature.

Media volume limit

Limit the maximum volume of the device when using Bluetooth speakers or headphones (not supplied).

1. In Settings, tap Sounds & vibrations> Volume.

2. Touch More Options> Media Volume Limit.

3. Touch to enable this feature.

- To adjust the maximum output volume, drag the Custom Volume Limit slider.

Ringtone

Adjust the ringtone by selecting preset sounds or adding your own.

1. In Settings, tap Sounds & vibrations> Ringtone.

2. Tap a ringtone to hear a preview and select it, or tap Add to use the sound file as a ringtone.

Notification sound

Select a preset sound for all alerts.

1. In Settings, tap Sounds & vibrations> Notification sound.

2. Touch a sound to hear a preview and select it.

Tip You can customize notification sounds to be unique for each application in the Application settings menu.

System Audio

Select the audio theme you want to use for touch interactions, charging, changing the sound mode and Samsung keyboard, and more.

In Settings, tap Sounds & vibrations> System sound and select an available option.

System Sounds and Vibrations

Adjust the device sounds and vibrations for actions such as tapping the screen and charging the device. Options may vary by operator.

○ In Settings, touch Sounds & vibration> System sound/vibration control for the following options:

Sound

• Touch interactions: Play tones when you tap or tap the screen to select.

• Charging: Play audio when the charger is connected.

• Dial keypad: Play a tone while dialing numbers on the phone keypad.

• Samsung keyboard: Play audio while typing with the Samsung keyboard. Vibrate

• Touch interactions: Vibrates when you tap the navigation keys or touch and hold items on the screen.

• Dial keypad: vibrates when dialing numbers on the telephone keypad.

• Navigation gestures: vibrate while using gestures.

• Charging: vibrates when the charger is connected.

• Samsung keyboard: vibrates when you type with the Samsung keyboard.

• Camera feedback: vibrate while taking a photo, zoom in, change shooting modes, and more.

Dolby Atmos

Enjoy Dolby Atmos quality when playing content that is specifically grouped for Atmos.

This function is only available with a connected headset.

In Settings, tap Sounds & vibrations> Sound quality and effects for the following options:

• Dolby Atmos: Experience a breakthrough in the sound that flows above you and around you.

• Dolby Atmos for gambling: use Dolby Atmos optimized for gambling.

Equalizer

Select a sound setting that is adapted to different music genres, or change the sound settings manually.

1. In Settings, tap Sounds & vibrations> Sound quality and effects.

2. Tap Equalizer to select a music genre.

UHQ upscale

Improve the resolution of music and video audio for a clearer listening experience.

 This function is only available with a connected headset.

1. In Settings, tap Sounds & vibrations> Sound quality and effects.

2. Touch the UHQ more upscale and select the zoom option.

Adjust the Sound

Adjust the sound to each ear and improve your listening experience.

1. In Settings, tap Sounds & vibrations> Sound quality and effects> Adjust sound.

2. Touch Adjust sound to choose when to change the sound settings.

3. Touch the sound profile that works best for you and tap Personalization settings. T

IP Touch Adjust the sound so that the device recognizes the best sound for you.

Separate Application Sound

You can select the application to play only the media sound in the Bluetooth speaker or headset separately from other sounds (for example, notifications).

To enable this option in the Audio device menu, connect to a Bluetooth device.

1. In Settings, tap Sounds & vibrations> Separate app sound.

2. Touch Turn on now to enable the app's separate sound, then set the following options:

• Application: Select an application to play audio on a separate audio device.

• Audio device: select the audio device on which you want to play the application sound.

Notifications

You can prioritize and simplify alerts for apps by changing the apps that send notifications and the way alerts alert you.

 Pop-up notification style

You can change the style and additional settings for notifications.

○ In the settings, tap Notifications, and then select a pop-up style:

• Short: This allows you to customize the notification colors, lighting style, and enabled apps.

- Included apps: View short notifications for your apps.

- Short pop-up settings: Adjust the Edge backlight style, colors, and enable notifications even when the screen is off.

Recently Sent Notifications

You can see a list of apps that have sent notifications under recently sent notifications.

1. In the settings, tap Notifications.

2. Touch the entry in the Recently Sent section to adjust the notification settings.

3. Touch More to display an expanded list.

Do Not Disturb

Do Not Disturb allows you to block sounds and notifications when this mode is on. You can also specify exceptions for people, programs, and alarms.

You can also set a schedule for recurring events such as sleep or appointments.

⚬ In Settings, click Notifications> Do Not Disturb and configure the following:

• Stop sounds and notifications.

• How long?: Select the default duration of Do Not Disturb mode if manually enabled.

• Sleep: Adjust Do Not Disturb mode during sleep.

• Add schedule: create a new schedule to set the day and time for regular device transfer in Do Not Disturb mode.

• Calls, messages, and conversations: Touch to enable Do Not Disturb exceptions.

• Alarms and sounds: enable sounds and vibrations for alarms, events, and reminders when Do Not Disturb mode is active.

• Applications: add applications from which you want to receive notifications in Do Not Disturb mode. You will still receive notifications of calls, messages, and conversations, even if you do not allow connected applications.

• Hide notifications: Review customization options to hide notifications.

Advanced settings

You can set notifications from applications and services.

○ In Settings, tap Notifications> Advanced Settings.

• Show notification icons: Change how many notifications appear in the status bar.

• Show battery charge percentage: Show the current life of your device in the status bar.

• Notification history: View recent and delayed notifications.

• Conversations: view conversation notifications. Touch and hold a conversation notification to prioritize it, set it to alert or silent.

• Floating notifications: enable floating notifications in balloons or a smart pop-up view.

• Suggest actions and replies to notifications: Get appropriate suggestions for actions regarding notifications and replies to messages.

• Notification reminders: Enable and customize occasional notification reminders for selected applications and services. To stop reminders, delete notifications.

• Application icon badges: Define which applications have active notifications with icons displayed on their icons. Touch to select whether the badges indicate the number of unread notifications.

• Wireless emergency alerts: personalize emergency notifications.

Alarm when the phone picks up,

you can set the device to notify you of missed calls and vibrate messages when you pick it up.

○ In Settings, tap Advanced Features> Gestures & Gestures> Alert when the phone rises to enable it.

CHAPTER EIGHTEEN

LOCK SCREEN AND SECURITY

Screen Lock Types

Biometric locks are also available to protect access to the device and sensitive data on the device.

Set A Secure Screen Lock

We recommend that you protect your device with a secure screen lock (form, PIN, or password). This is necessary to install and enable biometric locks.

1. In Settings, tap Lock screen> Screen lock type and tap Secure screen lock (pattern, PIN, or password).

2. Touch to display notifications on the lock screen. The following options are available:

• Icons only: Only notification icons are displayed in detail on the lock screen.

• Details: display details of notifications on the lock screen.

• Hide content: Do not show notifications on the Notification panel.

• Notifications to display: select which notifications are displayed on the lock screen.

• Always on display: Displays notifications on the Always on screen.

3. Configure the following screen lock options:

• Smart Lock: Unlocks the device automatically when it detects a trusted location or other device. This feature requires a secure screen lock.

• Secure lock settings: Adjust the secure lock settings. This feature requires a secure screen lock.

Clock and Information

You can configure features that appear on the lock screen, such as the clock and other useful information.

○ In the settings, tap Lock screen for the following options:

• Wallpaper services: Enable additional features such as a guide and a dynamic lock screen.

• Clock style: set the type and color of the clock on the lock screen and on the screen that is always on the screen.

• Hosting time: shows the time you are at home and while roaming.

• Gadgets: Enable gadgets on the lock screen and Always On Display for quick access to useful information.

• Contact information: View your contact information, such as a phone number or email address.

• Notifications: select notifications to be displayed on the lock screen and always on the screen.

• Shortcuts: Select shortcuts to the applications you want to add to the lock screen.

Google Play Protect

You can configure Google Play to regularly check your applications and device for security risks and threats.

◦ In Settings, click Biometrics & Security> Google Play Protect.

• Updates are checked automatically.

Security Update

You can easily check the date of the last installed security software to see if newer updates are available.

◌ In Settings, tap Biometrics & Security> Security Update to view the latest security update installed and make sure a newer update is available.

Find My Mobile

You can protect your device from loss or theft by locking, monitoring the network, and deleting data remotely.

You need a Samsung account, and you must turn on Google's location service before you can use Find My Mobile.

Turn on Find My Mobile

Before you can use Find My Mobile, you must turn it on and adjust your options.

1. In Settings, tap Biometrics & Security> Find my mobile phone.

2. Touch to enable Find My Mobile and log in to your Samsung account. The following options are available:

Samsung Pass

Use the Samsung Pass to access your favorite biometric services. You must log in to your Samsung account to use Samsung Pass.

1. In Settings, tap Biometrics & Security> Samsung Pass.

2. Log in to your Samsung account and add biometrics.

Protected Folder

You can create a secure folder on your device to protect your private content and applications from anyone who may be using your device.

 You must log in to your Samsung account to set up and use a secure folder.

○ In Settings, tap Biometrics & security> Folder protection and follow the instructions to protect the content on your device.

Secure Wi-Fi

When using unsecured Wi-Fi networks, provide additional privacy protection. You need to sign in to your Samsung account to set up and use a secure Wi-Fi network.

○ In Settings, tap Biometrics & Security> Secure Wi-Fi and follow the privacy settings.

Share Privately

Share files privately, prevent recipients from sharing them again, and set an expiration date.

○ In Settings, tap Biometrics & Security> Private Sharing and follow the instructions to add files.

Samsung BlockChain Keystone Manage your private blockchain key.

1. In Settings, tap Biometrics & Security> Samsung BlockChain Key Store.

2. Follow the instructions to import or set up a new cryptocurrency wallet.

Installing unknown applications

You can allow the installation of unknown third-party applications from selected applications or sources.

1. In Settings, tap Biometrics & Security> Install Unknown Apps.

2. Tap an application or source, and then tap Allow from this source.

Tip If you install unknown third-party programs, your device and personal information may become more exposed to security risks.

Factory Reset Password
You can request a factory reset password.

⚬ In Settings, click Biometrics & Security> Other Security Settings> Set / Change Password and enter your password.

Set a SIM card lock

You can set a PIN code to lock the SIM card to prevent unauthorized use of the SIM card if someone tries to use it on another device.

⚬ In Settings, press Biometrics & security> Other security settings> Set up SIM card lock and follow the instructions.

• Touch Lock SIM to turn on the feature.

• Touch Change SIM card Pin to create a new Pin code.

Displaying Passwords

Characters may be displayed briefly in the password fields when you enter them.

⚬ In Settings, tap Biometrics & security> Other security settings> Make passwords visible to turn on the feature.

Device Administration

You can grant security features and applications administrative access to your device.

1. In Settings, tap Biometrics & security> Other security settings> Device management apps.

2. Touch to turn it on as a device administrator.

Storing Credentials

You can manage trusted security certificates installed on your device that is authenticated on a secure connection server.

○ In Settings, tap Biometrics & security> Other security settings for the following options:

• Memory type: select where you want to save your credentials.

• Security certificate overview: View the certificates in the device ROM and other certificates that you have installed.

• User certificates: look at user certificates that identify your phone.

• Install from storage device/phone: install a new certificate from the repository.

• Delete credentials: Delete the contents of the credentials from the device and reset the password.

Advanced security settings Use these options to configure advanced security settings to better protect your device.

◌ In Settings, touch Biometrics & Security> Other Security Settings for the following options:

• Trusted Agents: Allow trusted devices to perform selected actions when connected.

- This option is displayed only when the lock screen is on.

• Pin windows: Pin an application to the device screen that prevents access to other device functions.

• Security policy updates: Protect your device by checking for security updates.

Permission Management

Applications can access the features of your device that you allow (such as cameras, microphones, or locations) when running in the background,

not just while using the application. You can set the device to notify you when this happens.

1. In Settings, tap Privacy> Permissions Manager.

2. Tap a category and then an app to select the permissions you want to be notified about.

NOTE The first time you use an application or service that wants to access certain features of your device, the dialog box asks if you want to allow it.

Samsung Privacy

If you have technical issues, send diagnostic information about your device to Samsung.

1. In the settings, tap Privacy.

2. In the Samsung section, tap the following customization options:

• Samsung Privacy: View Samsung's privacy information.

• Customization Service: Enable Samsung to provide customized content and recommendations.

• Send diagnostic information: If you have a technical problem, send diagnostic information about your device to Samsung.

Location

location services use GPS, mobile network, and Wi-Fi all together to get the location of your device.

1. In the settings, press Location.

2. Touch to turn on-location services.

TIP Some applications require you to turn on-location services for full functionality.

Application Permissions

Configure permissions for programs that want to access your location data.

1. In Settings, tap Location> Application Permissions.

2. Tap the application and select the permissions you want to assign. Options vary by application.

Improve Accuracy

Enable other location search tools.

1. In Settings, tap Location> Improve Accuracy.

2. Touch connection mode to add or remove location services:

• Wi-Fi overview: Allow apps and services to automatically search for Wi-Fi networks even when Wi-Fi is turned off.

• Bluetooth scan: Allow applications to automatically search for and connect to nearby devices via Bluetooth, even when Bluetooth is turned off.

Recent Location Requirements

1. In the settings, click Location.

2. Touch to turn on-location services.

3. Touch an entry in the Recent Location Requirements section to see the app settings.

Location Services

Location services use the latest information for your Phone. Some applications may use this information to improve search results based on the area you visit.

1. In the settings, click Location.

2. Touch an entry in the Location Services section to see how your location information is used.

CHAPTER NINETEEN

ACCOUNT AND DEVICE MAINTENANCE

You can connect to and manage accounts, including your Google Account, Samsung account, email, and social media accounts.

Add an Account

You can add and sync all email, social networking, and video and video accounts.

1. In Settings, touch Accounts & Backups> Account Management> Add Account.

2. Touch one of the account types.

3. Follow the instructions to enter your credentials and set up your account.

- Touch Automatic data synchronization to enable automatic account updates.

Account settings

Each account has its custom settings.

○ In Settings, tap Accounts & Backups> Manage Accounts.

Deleting an account

You can remove accounts from your device.

1. In Settings, tap Accounts & Backups> Manage Accounts.

2. Press an account, and then click erase the account.

Backup and Recovery

You can configure your device to back up data to personal accounts.

Samsung account

You can enable data backup on your Samsung account.

○ In Settings, tap Accounts & Backup> Backup & Restore for options in Samsung Cloud:

• Data Backup: Configure your Samsung account for data backup.

• Restore data: Restore data backups with your Samsung account.

Google Account

You can enable data backup in your Google Account.

1. In the settings, tap Accounts & backups.

2. In the Google Drive section, tap Data backup.

Transferring External Memory

You can use the smart switch to back up data to a USB memory device or backups.

◌ In Settings, tap Accounts & Backups> Transfer External Memory.

Google Settings

You can adjust Google settings for your device. The options available depend on your Google Account.

◌ In the settings, tap Google and select a customization option.

DEVICE MAINTENANCE

Quick optimization

The quick optimization feature improves device performance by doing the following:

• Identifying applications that consume too much power and removing unnecessary items from memory.

• Delete unnecessary files and close programs running in the background.

• Malware scan. To use the Quick Optimizer feature:

◌ In Settings, tap Battery and device care> Optimize now.

Battery

See how the battery is used for different activities of the device.

◌ In Settings, tap Battery and device> Battery for the following options:

• Last used: View recent battery life by time, application, and service.

• Background restrictions: View programs that you do not use often, and limit their battery consumption. To disable this feature, tap Sleep unused apps.

• Wireless power-sharing: Enable wireless charging of supported devices with the device battery.

• More battery settings: - Flexible battery: Limit battery consumption for programs you don't use often.

- Improved processing: speed up data processing for the most demanding applications and games. This option consumes more battery power.

- Show battery charge percentage: Display the battery charge percentage next to the battery icon in the status bar.

- Show charge information: shows the battery charge level and the estimated time until it is charged when Always On Display is off or not displayed.

- Fast charging: Enable or disable fast charging of the cable when it is connected to a supported charger.

- Superfast charge: Enable or disable super-fast charge if connected to a charger.

Storage

Browse your capabilities and detailed usage by file categories and types.

⊚ In Settings, tap Battery and device care> Storage.

• Touch a category to view and manage files.

Memory

Check the amount of available memory. You can close background applications and reduce the amount of memory that you use to speed up the device.

⊚ In Settings, tap Battery & device> Memory. The used and available memory is displayed.

• Touch Clear Now to free up as much memory as possible.

• Touch Show more to see a complete list of programs and services that use memory.

Touch to turn these apps and services on or off.

• Touch apps that have not been used recently to view apps and services included in this group.

Touch to turn these apps and services on or off.

• Touch Excluded apps to display a list of excluded apps.

Touch Add apps to select the apps you want to exclude from memory usage checks.

Advanced device care options

Other Phone care features are there in the menu.

In the settings, tap Battery and device. The following options are available:

• Search: locate panels that are installed or available for installation.

• Care Report: Review information on restart history and charging and temperature tips.

• More options: - Show icon on the application screen: Displays the device care icon on the application screen.

- Automation: automatically optimize your device at a specific time according to your usage patterns.

- About device care: See version and license information about the device care feature.

CHAPTER TWENTY

LANGUAGE AND INPUT

Configure the input language and settings on your device.

Change the device language

You can add languages to the list and organize them as you wish. If the app does not support your default language, it will switch to the next supported language in your list.

1. In Settings, tap General Management> Language.

2. Touch Add language and select a language from the list.

3. Touch Set as default to change the device language.

• To switch to another language in the list, tap the language you want, then tap Apply.

Convert Text to Speech

○ In the settings, tap General management> Convert text to speech for options:

• Preferred mechanism: select Samsung or Google text-to-speech. Touch Options settings.

• Language: set the default speech-language.

• Tone: adjust the pitch.

• Playback: Touch to play a short speech synthesis display.

• Reset: reset the speed and pitch of the speech.

Keyboard list and defaults

Change the default keyboard, change the built-in keyboards, and change the keyboard settings.

◌ In Settings, tap General Control> Keyboard List and Default for the following options:

• Default Keyboard: Select the default keyboard for device menus and keyboards.

• Samsung keyboard: change Samsung keyboard settings.

• Google Voice Typing: Change Google Voice input settings.

• Samsung voice input: change Samsung voice input settings.

• Navigation bar keyboard button: Enable the navigation bar button to quickly switch between keyboards.

Physical keyboards

Customize options when you connect a physical keyboard to the device (sold separately).

1. In the settings, tap General Management.

2. Touch Physical Keyboard and select an option:

• Show On-Screen Keyboard: Display the on-screen keyboard while using the physical keyboard.

• Shortcut keys: Displays keyboard shortcut explanations on the screen.

Mouse and Touchpad

Configure the cursor speed and button assignments for the optional mouse or Touchpad (not included).

In Settings, tap General Control> Mouse & Touchpad.

• In the Cursor Speed section, drag the slider to the right to move faster or to the left to move more slowly.

• Touch the Primary button and select Left or Right.

Autofill Service

Save time when entering data with autocomplete services.

1. In the settings, tap General Management.

2. Touch AutoFill to display the selected service.

- Touch Settings to customize your service.

- Touch AutoFill to change the default service.

Date and Time

By default, the device receives date and time information from the wireless network. Outside network coverage, you can set the date and time manually.

In Settings, click General Management> Date & Time. The following options are available:

• Automatic date and time: Get date and time updates on the wireless network. When automatic date and time is disabled, these options are available:

- Select time zone: select a new time zone.

- Set date: enter the current date.

- Set time: Enter the current time.

• Use 24-hour format time show.

Personalization Service

Samsung devices, applications, and services are designed to provide you with personalized services with smart and intelligent anticipation of your wishes and needs.

○ In Settings, tap General Management> Personalization Service.

Troubleshooting

You can check for software updates and, if necessary, reset the services on your device.

Software updates

Check and install available software updates for your device. Options may vary by operator.

○ In the settings, click Software update for these options:

• Find updates: manually search for software updates.

• Continue update: Continue with the interrupted update.

• View software update history: View a list of all software updates on your device.

• Smart updates: Install security updates automatically.

• Use the Software Update Assistant: Connect your device to a computer to use the Software Update Assistant.

• Last update: View information about installing the current software.

• PRL update: Download and install the Preferred Roaming List update.

• Update profile: Automatically update the user profile information.

• UICC unlock: enable the SIM slot to use another operator's card. Contact your operator for assistance.

Reset All Settings

You can reset the phone to the factory settings, except security, language, and account settings. Personal data is not affected.

1. In Settings, tap General Management> Cancel> Clear All Settings.

2. Touch Reset Settings and confirm when prompted.

Resetting Network Settings

You can reset your Wi-Fi, mobile data, and Bluetooth settings by resetting your network settings.

1. In Settings, tap General Management> Reset> Reset Network Settings.

2. Touch Reset Settings and confirm when prompted.

Reset Accessibility Settings

You can reset the accessibility settings of your device. This does not affect the accessibility settings in downloaded applications and your personal information.

1. In Settings, click General Management> Cancel> Clear Availability Settings.

2. Touch Reset Settings and confirm when prompted.

Restart Automatically At Specified Hours

Optimize your device to restart automatically at specified hours. All unsaved data will be lost after restarting the device.

1. In Settings, tap General Management> Reset> Automatic Restart at a specified time.

2. Touch to turn on the automatic restart, then set the following parameters:

• Days: select the day of the week to restart the device automatically.

• Time: set the time when you want to restart the device.

Restore Factory Data

You can restore the device to the factory settings by deleting all data.

This action permanently deletes ALL data from your device, including Google or other account settings, system and application data, and settings, downloaded apps such as music, pictures, videos, and other files.

When you sign in to your Google Account on your device, the factory default security (FRP) is turned on. It protects the phone against loss or theft. If you reset your device to the factory default settings with FRP enabled, you'll need to enter your registered Google Account username and password to re-access your device. You will not be able to access the device without the appropriate credentials.

NOTE If you reset the password for your Google Account, it can take up to 24 hours for the password reset to sync with all devices registered in the account.

Before resetting the device:

1. Make sure that the data you want to keep is transferred to your repository.

2. Log in to your Google Account and verify your username and password.

To reset the device:

1. In Settings, tap General Management> Cancel> Restore Factory Defaults.

2. Touch Reset and follow the reset instructions.

3. When the device restarts, follow the instructions to set up the device.

Factory default security When you log in to your Google Account on your device, factory default security (FRP) is activated.

For example, if you lose or steal your device and reset it to factory settings,

it can only be used by someone with a Google Account username and password.

After resetting to factory settings, you won't be able to access your device unless you have a username and password for your Google Account.

Caution Before sending your device to Samsung or taking it to an authorized Samsung service center, remove your Google Account and then reset it to factory settings.

Enabling factory settings protection

When you add a Google Account to your device, the FRP security feature is automatically activated.

Disable factory settings protection To disable FRP, remove all Google Accounts from your device.

1. In Settings, touch Accounts & Backups> Account Management> [Google Account].

2. Touch Remove Account.

Collecting diagnostics

Collect diagnostic data to troubleshoot problems. Options may vary by operator.

○ In Settings, tap General Management> Cancel> Collect Diagnostics. The following options are available:

• Device data collection: Help solve device problems.

CHAPTER TWENTY-ONE

ACCESSIBILITY

There are accessibility settings for people who need help viewing, hearing, or otherwise operating their device.

Accessibility services are special features that make it easier for everyone to use the device

Recommended for you

See a list of accessibility features that you use and some of the recommended features that you may want to enable.

○ In Settings, tap Accessibility> Recommended seeing recommendations.

Talkback

Use special controls and settings that allow you to navigate without having to display the screen.

1. In Settings, tap Accessibility> Talkback.

2. Touch to enable the feature, then touch the customization options:

- Talkback shortcut: Select a shortcut to quickly turn on Talkback.

- Settings: Configure Talkback settings to help you better.

Visibility Enhancements

You can configure accessibility features to help with the visual aspects of your device.

Colours and Clarity

 You can adjust the colors and contrast of text and other display elements for easy viewing.

○ In Settings, tap Accessibility> Visibility enhancements, and then:

• High contrast theme: Adjust screen and font colors to increase contrast for easier viewing.

• High contrast fonts: Adjust the color and outline of the fonts to increase the contrast with the background.

• Highlight buttons: display buttons with shaded backgrounds to make them stand out better in the background.

• Color inversion: Convert a color screen from white text on a black background to black text on a white background.

• Adjust color: Adjust the color of the screen if you have difficulty seeing certain colors.

• Add color filter: adjust screen colors if you have trouble reading text.

• Remove animations: If you are sensitive to movement, remove some screen effects.

Size and Zoom

You can increase the size of supported display items and create shortcuts to features for people with disabilities on your device.

○ In Settings, tap Accessibility> Visibility enhancements, and then tap:

• Magnifier window: Zoom in on the content displayed on the screen.

• Zoom: Use excessive gestures such as triple-tap, double-tap, and drag two fingers across the screen.

• Large mouse pointer / Touchpad: Use the large mouse pointer or Touchpad (optional).

• Font size and style: set the fonts on the screen.

• Screen magnification: set the screen magnification level.

Hearing Enhancements

You can set up features for people with disabilities to help with the audio aspects of your device. Options may vary by operator.

Sounds

You can adjust the sound quality when using hearing aids or headphones.

In Settings, tap Accessibility> Hearing Enhancements, and then tap:

• Real-time text: Activate real-time call (RTT).

• Hearing aid support: Improve the sound quality to listen better with hearing aids.

• Increase ambient sound: Enable this feature and connect headphones to the device to amplify conversation sounds.

• Adjust the sound: Adjust the sound to each ear and improve your listening experience. See Adjust the sound.

• Left / Right balance: Use the slider to adjust the left and right balance while listening to stereo sound.

• Mono sound: Switch the sound from stereo to mono when using one headset.

• Mute all sounds: Mute all notifications and sounds for privacy.

Display text

While watching multimedia, you can convert speech to text and view captions.

◌ In Settings, tap Accessibility> Hearing Enhancements, and then tap:

• Live transcript: Record speech and convert it to text with the microphone.

• Live captions: automatically subtitle the speech in the media played on your device.

• Google Subtitles (CC): Configure subtitle and subtitle services.

• Audible notifications: Receive alerts when a device detects a baby crying or a doorbell.

Interaction and skill

You can configure accessibility features to help with limited skills when interacting with your device.

Alternate input

You can control the device with different types of inputs and controls.

◌ In Settings, tap Accessibility> Interaction & Skill, then tap:

• Universal switch: Control your device with custom switches.

• Assistant menu: Improve the accessibility of the device for users with reduced skill.

Interactions

You can simplify the gestures required to receive phone calls or answer notifications and alarms.

⊙ In Settings, tap Accessibility> Interaction & Skills, then tap:

• Answer and end calls: - Read caller names aloud: Listen aloud to caller names if you use Bluetooth or a headset (sold separately).

- Automatic answer: answer a call after a specified time when using a Bluetooth or headset (sold separately).

- Press the volume key to answer: use the volume keys to answer calls.

- To end a call, press the side key: To end the call, press the side key.

• Interaction control: customize the areas of interaction on the screen, keyboard, and keyboard.

Touch settings

You can adjust the screen to make it less sensitive to touches and touches.

○ In Settings, tap Accessibility> Interaction & Skill, then tap:

• Touch & hold delay: Select a time interval for this action.

• Touch duration: set how long the interaction should take to be recognized as a touch.

• Ignore repetitive touches: set the time at which repeated touches will be ignored.

Mouse and physical keyboard

Configure settings for the connected mouse and physical keyboard.

○ In Settings, tap Accessibility> Interaction & Skill and touch:

• Auto-click after stopping the cursor: Automatically click an item when the cursor stops on it.

• Sticky keys: When you press a modification key, such as Shift, Ctrl, or Alt, the key remains pressed and allows you to enter shortcut keys by pressing one key at a time.

Slow keys: Set how long a key is held down before you recognize it as a keypress, which helps prevent accidental keystrokes.

• Reject keys: set how long to wait before you accept another key, press to prevent the same key from being accidentally pressed repeatedly. Advanced settings You can customize additional features and services to access your device.

Tip You can download additional apps for people with disabilities from the Google Play store.

Accessibility shortcuts ◌ In Settings, tap Accessibility> Advanced settings, and then:

• Accessibility button: Select a shortcut to access the accessibility button.

• Side keys and volume keys: Set the selected functions for people with disabilities by pressing the side keys and volume keys at the same time.

• Volume up and down keys: Configure the selected services to activate when you press and hold the volume up and down keys for three seconds.

Notifications ○ In Settings, tap Accessibility> Advanced settings, and then tap:

• Flash notification: Camera or screen flashes or lights when you receive notifications or when an alarm sounds.

• Action time: Select how long messages that require you to take action but are only temporarily visible (for example, notifications) are displayed.

• Speak aloud the keyboard entry: the device will read aloud what you type on the keyboard.

• Bixby Vision for accessibility: add ways to read text aloud, describe scenes, discover colors, and more.

• Voice tag: record voice recordings to NFC tags (not included) to provide information about objects or locations near them.

Installed Services

You can install additional help services for your device.

○ In Settings, tap Accessibility> Installed Services.

NOTE After installation, additional accessibility services are listed and configured here.

About accessibility

Legal and license information for the current accessibility software is available in Settings.

◌ In Settings, tap Accessibility> About accessibility. The following information is available:

• Version: View the current version of the software for people with disabilities.

• Open Source Licenses: View information about open source licenses used for accessibility.

CHAPTER TWENTY-TWO

OTHER APPS

Configure features on your Phone that makes it simple to use.

Android Auto

Android Auto brings the most helpful apps to your Phone screen as well as to a compatible car screen in a way that makes it very simple for you to focus on driving. You can control functions such as navigation and maps, calls and text messages, and music.

Connect your device

Before you connect your device for the first time, turn on the car and allow time to set up Android Auto.

1. Connect the USB cable to the USB port in the vehicle and the other end of the cable to the device.

2. Your device may prompt you to download the Android Auto app or update it to the latest version of the app.

3. Select Android Auto on the car screen and adhere to the instructions.

Note The Bluetooth in your device turns on automatically when Android Auto is connected to the car via USB.

Connectivity Help

Browse connected vehicles, connect new vehicles, and find Android Auto technical support.

◦ In Settings, tap Advanced Features> Android Auto for the following features:

• Connect your car: Follow the instructions to connect your device to a compatible USB port in your vehicle or Android Auto wireless.

• Connection Help: See the Android Auto Help support page.

• Previously connected cars: View the accepted and rejected cars that your device has connected to.

Tip click More options> Forget all cars to erase all accepted and rejected cars from the Phone.

General

Customize settings for Android Auto.

◦ In Settings, tap Advanced Features> Android Auto for the following features:

• Customize Launcher: Choose when apps will appear in Android Auto and how they will appear in the car screen launcher.

• "Hey Google" detection: Log in to your Google account and enable voice commands for hands-free calling.

• Auto resume media: Enable this option to automatically resume media playback when you start driving.

• Google Now: set the weather, home, work, and more for Google Now.

• Weather: Enable this option to display weather information on the car screen obtained from the location of your device.

Notifications

Select how to display incoming notifications.

In Settings, tap Advanced features> Android Auto for the following features:

• View incoming messages: Enable the first line of the incoming notification if your car is stopped.

• Show message notifications: Receive notifications of new messages while driving.

• Show group message notifications: Receive notifications of new group messages while driving.

• No notification sound: enable this option to receive notification sounds while driving.

System

Adjust system settings for Android Auto. ◌ In Settings, tap Advanced Features> Android Auto for the following features:

• Wireless Android Auto: Can pair your Phone with cars without a USB cable.

• Google Analytics: Enable the use of this Google Analytics application for background crash reporting and usage statistics (application restart required).

About

View the latest information on Android Auto legislation, security, privacy, and licenses.

◌ In Settings, tap Advanced Features> Android Auto for the following features:

• Security, data, and legal notices: important information about security and Android Auto.

• Version: View version information and permissions for Android Auto.

Tips and help

See tips and techniques, and a user guide for your device.

○ In the settings, tap Tips and help. Dual Messenger Use two separate accounts for the same program.

1. In Settings, tap Advanced Features> Dual Messenger.

2. Click next to apps to enable the feature for each app.

- To select which contacts will have access to the secondary messaging application, tap Use a separate contact list.

About Your Phone

Look for information about your phone, including current status, legal information, hardware, software versions, and more.

1. In Settings, click About Phone to look at your phone number, model number, serial number, and IMEI information.

2. Touch additional items to see more information about your device.

TIP You can view the FCC device ID in About Phone> Status Information.

INDEX